Oracle Hyperion Financial Reporting 11

A Practical Guide

Edward J. Cody

Eric M. Somers

P 8
tech

Published in 2015 by P8tech, an imprint of Play Technologies (England) Limited

Copyright © Play Technologies (England) Limited

ISBN: 978-0-9574105-3-4

P8Tech
6 Woodside
Churnet View Road
Oakamoor
ST10 3AE

www.P8Tech.com

About the Authors

Edward J. Cody is a subject matter expert in planning/budgeting, data warehouse, and business intelligence systems with over ten years of experience with Oracle EPM, BI, and database technology. He is the author of *The Business Analyst's Guide to Oracle Hyperion Interactive Reporting 11*, the *Oracle Hyperion Interactive Reporting 11 Expert Guide*, and *The Oracle Data Relationship Management 11 Guide: Successful Implementation Essentials*. He has spoken on Hyperion EPM, Oracle BI, and mobile security at Oracle OpenWorld, OTDUG Kaleidoscope, OAUG Collaborate, and regional user groups. He is an Oracle Certified Implementation Specialist in Oracle Hyperion Planning 11, Oracle Essbase 11, Oracle Business Intelligence Foundation Suite 11g, and Oracle 11g Data Warehousing.

Edward has consulted to both private and public sector organizations throughout his career, implementing and managing solutions across the United States and Europe. He has a Bachelor of Science in Systems Engineering from George Washington University's School of Engineering and Applied Science, and a Master of Science in Management of Information Technology from the University of Virginia's McIntire School of Commerce. His experience includes leading one of the largest commercial Oracle EPM and BI shared services organizations, and he is currently leading Oracle and financial management consulting engagements for the Definitive Logic Corporation.

Eric M. Somers has worked with information systems for the last 10 years in both private and public sector organizations. He has spent the last 4 years working directly with Oracle Hyperion Financial Reporting in support of Oracle Essbase, Oracle Hyperion Planning, and Oracle Hyperion Financial Management (HFM) projects. He has a Bachelor of Science in Decision Sciences & Management Information Systems from George Mason University's School of Management, and a Master of Business Administration from Strayer University. He has consulted to both private and public sector organizations throughout his career, and he is currently working with the Definitive Logic Corporation on Oracle EPM and BI engagements.

Acknowledgements

Eric Somers and Edward Cody would like to thank everyone who purchased this book. We hope that it serves as a great resource and aid in your use of the product and ongoing development activities. We would also like to thank the reviewers for their time and attention to this material. Heartfelt thanks to James Lumsden-Cook and all of those at P8tech Publishing for their mentorship and efforts to bring the material to print. They are a wonderful group and we look forward to their continued growth in the technical publishing space.

About the Reviewers

Elisabeth Flores is a Senior Enterprise Performance Management and Business Intelligence developer with over 5 years of experience working with Oracle Hyperion and Business Intelligence software. She specializes in Oracle Hyperion Planning and Essbase deployments, and she has extensive experience in integrating Oracle BI with Hyperion applications. She is an Oracle Certified Implementation Specialist in Oracle Hyperion Planning 11, Oracle Essbase 11, Oracle Business Intelligence Foundation Suite 11g. She holds a Bachelor of Science in Information Systems and Operations Management from George Mason University. She is currently consulting and supporting customers in the US and Europe with their Oracle Hyperion projects.

Katie (Bowers) La Celle currently works as a Business Intelligence and Enterprise Performance Management technical architect, project manager, and senior developer. She has extensive experience with the Oracle EPM and BI product suites, and is an Oracle Certified Specialist in Hyperion Planning, Oracle Essbase, and Oracle Business Intelligence. Her specialty is Hyperion Planning with currency translation, and she enjoys working on complex Hyperion Planning implementations. She has had the opportunity to lead Hyperion development for customers across Canada, the UK, Italy, Spain, and the United States.

Michelle M. Pham is a Senior BI/EPM Engineer with over 10 years of experience with data warehousing, Oracle BI, and Hyperion products. She specializes in Oracle Hyperion Data Relationship Management, Essbase, Planning, Interactive Reporting, and data warehouse projects, and she has consulted for the U.S. Federal Government and private-sector clients. She co-presented with Edward J. Cody at KScope and Collaborate on the Success with DRM at General Dynamics. She holds a Bachelor of Science in Information Technology and a Bachelor of Science in Decision Sciences & Management Information Systems from George Mason University. She is also an Oracle Certified Implementation Specialist through Oracle University.

Katharine E. Rehm has worked with information systems for the last 3 years in private sector organizations. She works directly with Oracle Hyperion Financial Reporting in support of Oracle Essbase, Oracle Hyperion Planning, and Oracle Hyperion Financial Management (HFM) projects. She has a Bachelor of Science in Accounting from the George Mason University's School of Business, and she is currently working on a budgeting, forecasting and external reporting team for a large publically traded company.

Preface

Oracle Hyperion Financial Reporting is the business intelligence and reporting software package bundled within Oracle's Enterprise Performance Management software. The product provides the ability to report from Oracle Essbase, Oracle Hyperion Planning, and Oracle Hyperion Financial Management (HFM) applications easily. The software provides the means to build reporting templates for individual execution or package FR Books or FR Batches with dynamic content, prompts, and calculations.

This book examines the power of the Financial Reporting software product covering basic operations to advanced techniques. The book works through the development of a simple grid, use of suppression, conditional formulas, functions and formulas, books and batches, and even integration with Smart View. Examples are provided to demonstrate the capabilities discussed based on personal experiences with the product.

What you need for this book

This book was written using a standard deployment of Oracle EPM 11.1.2.3.500 on a Windows 2008R2 server with an Oracle 11gR2 database. The sections and techniques in this book are primarily version independent, and almost all of the demonstrated functionality exists in previous versions of the product. The book leverages the ASO Sample Essbase application for the examples provided. All reports were designed by the authors during the creation of the book.

Installing the Software

Oracle has recently released software guides for completing rapid installations. The software installation for this book was completed following a guide similar to the Rapid Deployment of Oracle Hyperion Planning in Development Environments found in the Oracle online documentation. Following this documentation provides the steps needed to stand-up a local Hyperion installation with Planning, Essbase, and Financial Reporting software.

Who this book is for

The target audience of this book is business and technical users looking to learn report building techniques. The book focuses on the product features, common business techniques, and information needed to be successful with the product on a day-to-day basis.

Table of Contents

Chapter 3 – Grids: Basic Operations, Charting, and the Point of View

Chapter 4 – Grids: Basic Formatting

Chapter 5 – Grids: Advanced Member Selection & Formulas

Chapter 6 – Conditional Formatting

Chapter 7 – Suppression and Conditional Suppression

Chapter 8 – Advanced Techniques

Chapter 9 – Report Templates and Text Label Functions

Chapter 10 – Financial Reporting Books

Chapter 11 – Financial Reporting Batches

Chapter 12 – Oracle Smart View Integration with Financial Reporting

1

Introducing Oracle Hyperion Financial Reporting

Welcome to the first published book on Oracle Hyperion Financial Reporting! The focus of this book is to address the needs of power-users, developers, and users looking to gain further information on the product. Our goal is to educate readers on the features of Financial Reporting and to provide developers with advanced report building techniques including calculations and multiple grids, alongside other formulas and examples not documented in the product manuals. This book does not repeat the content of the user's manual, but rather teach the best-practices and techniques used by experts when developing reports.

Through our learning and use of the Financial Reporting product, we know that there are many ways to design, develop, and format reports. Many methods add complexity and require significant maintenance, driving poor performance and significant time investment. We have identified a set of approaches that we feel is best for the development and maintenance of reports based on our experience using the product. Over the next set of chapters, we demonstrate our experience with the product and highlight the features, approaches, and methodologies needed to succeed with the Oracle Hyperion Financial Reporting software.

The following content is introduced in this chapter:

- Oracle Hyperion Financial Reporting Introduction
- The EPM Workspace
- Running Financial Reports
- Financial Reporting Studio

What is Oracle Hyperion Financial Reporting?

Oracle Hyperion Financial Reporting is one of the many reporting tools used to report from Hyperion Essbase, Hyperion Planning, and Hyperion Financial Management (HFM). While this product may seem common in a sea of other similar reporting technologies, Oracle Hyperion Financial Reporting has a very specific role in Oracle's Analytics strategy today. Most people that we come across believe Financial Reporting is another tool headed for the graveyard. However, while other Hyperion reporting products are to be retired, you may be surprised to find that the recent release of Oracle Business Intelligence software includes Financial Reporting. With the ability to produce books and batches, annotations and cell-text integration, as well as XBRL, Oracle Hyperion Financial Reporting is a common utility used by most organizations for building and distributing briefing packages, collaborating on financial metrics, and servicing mobile and paper-based reporting.

Exciting News (OBIEE 11.1.1.7)

Oracle Hyperion Financial Reporting is now a part of Oracle Business Intelligence Enterprise Edition. Not only was Financial Reporting released with OBIEE 11.1.1.7, so was Essbase and a light version of Workspace utilized for running Financial Reports in an integrated framework with the Oracle BI toolset. This is the first release of a Hyperion and Oracle BI software product together post the Hyperion buyout and a major step forward in bringing the Oracle BI and Oracle Hyperion EPM software together.

Oracle Hyperion Disclosure Management & XBRL

An important feature of Financial Reporting is its integration with Oracle Hyperion Disclosure Management. Extensible Business Reporting Language (XBRL) has been a major buzzword used in many marketing briefings for Financial Reporting for the past few years. XBRL is based on XML and was designed as a framework to support financial information sharing. Submitting financial statements using XBRL is completed by companies for certain SEC filings or used by banks when submitting information to the FDIC and other various scenarios. The use of XBRL in financial information sharing continues to take shape across the financial reporting landscape.

The Oracle Hyperion Disclosure Management product is used specifically for creating and managing XBRL content in the enterprise. The product integrates with Microsoft Word, Excel, and Financial Reporting. We feel this integration and the ability to broker XBRL tagged content is another area of expansion for the use of Financial Reporting in organizations.

Mobility

Oracle has made major strides over the past few years on their mobile technology and mobility across business intelligence. Part of the strategy is from both a mobile application perspective as well as a browser-based rendering perspective. While there is no mobile application at this time, Financial Reporting can now be viewed using the Safari browser on Apple mobile devices. Future plans have also been released for a mobile application for Hyperion Planning. It is exciting to see the future evolution of mobility as it relates to Financial Reporting. For more information in relation to mobility, view the new Oracle Hyperion Financial Reporting Mobile User's Guide located with the Oracle EPM 11.1.2.3 documentation.

Getting Started with FR

What do I need to know to get started? This book does not require an extensive background on Oracle Hyperion Financial Reporting to get you started with the software. However, having a Hyperion deployment post version 9 with Workspace, Essbase, Planning, and Smart View will help you better understand the information provided throughout the book. Many people ask, "Is Hyperion 11.1.2.3 different from other versions of the software since System 9?" While there are new features and additional benefits to using the new software, most of the functionality that is leveraged in daily use with the software remains the same across versions. Whether you are on the newest version of the software, on Hyperion 11.1.1.3, or even on Hyperion 9.3, this book is relevant and serves as a useful tool for learning about the software product.

Installing Oracle EPM 11.1.2.3

In our opinion, user-driven books that begin with a large section on installing the software product are not commonly geared to the user community. While installing a server deployment of the product is required for Financial Reporting, most users and even developers typically do not play a role in installing and maintaining an enterprise deployment. Even though we do not discuss installing the product throughout the chapters of the book, we have referenced the documentation used for the installation in the preface of the book.

For those interested in learning about installations, the software has become much easier to install over the past few versions. The Oracle EPM rapid install guides are great references for quickly installing the features utilized throughout this book. Please visit the section on installing the software in the preface to gather more information on server installations. Later in this chapter, we discuss the installation of the Financial Reporting Studio product, which is the client tool that is used to create and manage reports.

The EPM Workspace

"I thought this book was about Oracle Hyperion Financial Reporting. Why are we starting with Workspace?" Commonly, we are asked, "What is the Workspace? Is Workspace a portal?" The response to this question is complicated, because the EPM Workspace is the central access point to nearly all Oracle EPM content for the user community outside of the content accessible via Smart View.

However, Workspace is much more than a portal, especially when it comes to Financial Reporting. Workspace is an engine that allows users of the software to create reporting books and batches, execute reports across points of view, and provide access to report output. Financial Reporting is one of many products that integrate with Workspace, providing users with a central location to save, share, and publish content. It is important to understand the features of Workspace when using and/or developing in Financial Reporting.

The HomePage

The typical starting point for the EPM Workspace is the login page. The following screenshot shows the login page for the Oracle EPM 11.1.2.3 Workspace.

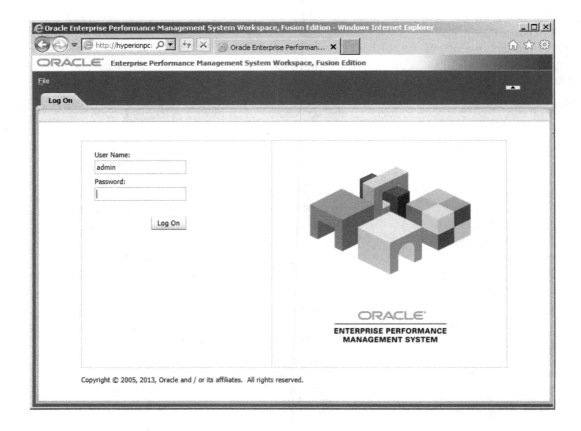

> Notice in the screenshot above, the login used was the administrator account for the system. The administrator account contains full permissions to the system, and your individual access may be limited based on your specific configuration.

In most environments, Workspace opens to the **HomePage**, providing recently opened documents, quick links, and defined Workspace pages. The following image shows an example of the EPM Workspace main screen.

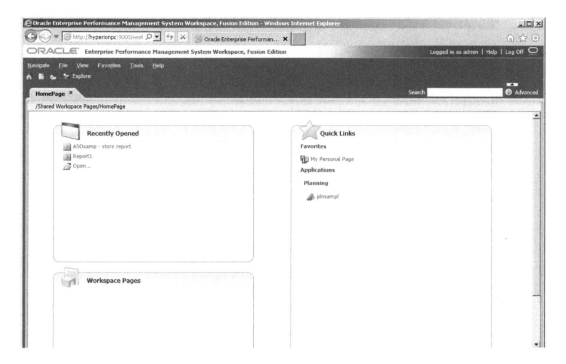

Workspace Menu Bar

Workspace includes many useful toolbars displayed at the top of the screen. The following screenshot shows the menu toolbar that is part of the standard Workspace screen:

The **Menu Bar**, the bar that starts with the Navigate menu, contains the following menu items:

- **Navigate** - The Navigate menu now replaces the navigate wheel that was used in prior versions of the software. The Navigate menu provides the ability to navigate through different application objects as well as features and administrative tools in the product set. It is especially important when scheduling jobs in Financial Reporting as the scheduler is accessed from the menu.

- **File** – The File menu displays options which are common to any file menu, including Open, Save, etc. More importantly, the File menu contains the *Preferences* menu item which contains specific Financial Reporting configuration settings. Setting Financial Reporting preferences is discussed in the next section of this chapter.

- **View** - The View menu provides the ability to show and hide the different panes of Workspace.
- **Favorites** - The Favorites menu provides the ability to manage your favorites and provides access to your personal page.
- **Tools** - The Tools menu varies across the different sections of Workspace and provides links to install the desktop components associated with the software. It also contains a link to install and launch the Financial Reporting Studio.
- **Help** – The Help menu provides links to software documentation.

> Workspace menus may change based on your location in the application. Relevant menu changes are addressed later in the book.

Workspace Shortcut Toolbar

The toolbar below the menu contains a few shortcut buttons that are helpful when using Workspace. The Menu bar includes the home button, new file, open, and explore options shown in the following screenshot.

Additionally, the far right-hand side of the page contains an upgraded **Search** option. Above the search section is a small button that allows you to hide toolbars for extra screen space, an especially useful feature when using Financial Reporting or any of the applications within Workspace.

Exploring Workspace (Explore)

The **Explore** window, shown in the following screenshot, opens a page with two panes: a folder structure on the left for navigating the file structure and the contents of the current folder on the right for managing, provisioning, and executing objects. The following screenshot is open to the default view of the Explore window:

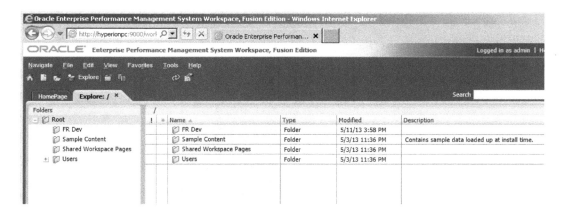

As items are opened in Workspace, tabs are created at the top of the screen (in previous versions the tabs were opened at the bottom of the screen). Users navigate through the different locations by clicking on the tab names, and tabs can be closed by clicking the X or right-clicking on the tab and selecting Close. The Explore window shows metadata about each report and folder in Workspace. In a similar fashion to Windows, clicking on the header of the main Explore window displays a list of additional metadata that may be shown in Workspace including the Version, Owner, Created, and Size of the document. The following screenshot shows the right-click menu to show or hide the different options in the main Explore window.

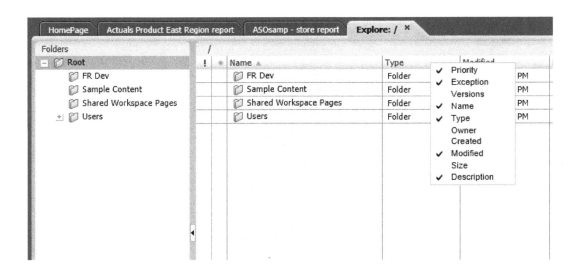

Financial Reporting Preferences

When using Financial Reporting, a section exists in Workspace for setting specific preferences for each user. These preferences are specific to each user throughout the use of the application. The following screenshot shows the Financial Reporting Preferences window.

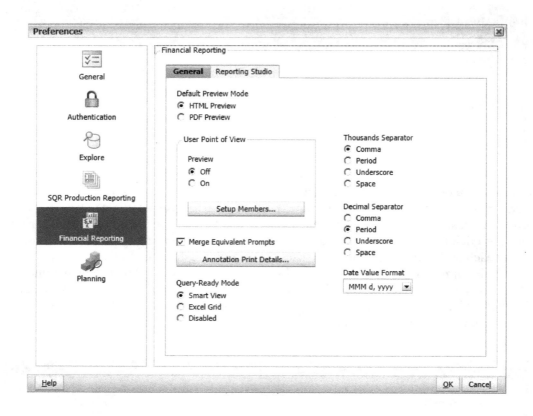

The first section of the preferences window provides the ability for the user to change the default preview output when double-clicking on a report. The default is HTML but many users prefer the PDF display option as the primary display option. The second major section of the menu is the configuration of the User Point of View.

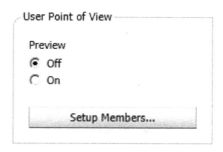

Most users set the User Point of View preview to On. The on setting allows users to select the user-prompted values during report runtime. Running reports with the preview set to off may result in an error message when opening reports. If a user chooses not to display the prompt screen during runtime, there is a button to setup members for the Point of View. Each of these preference settings is driven by the database connection and can be used to define user-specific preferences for dimension values. The following chapters address the features and configuration of the User Point of View.

Continuing with the preference settings, other useful formatting options exist on the right-hand side of the window. The features include setting Thousands and Decimal formatting as well as Date Value Format. At the bottom of the window, settings exist for the execution of **Query-Ready Mode**. Query-Ready Mode is an incredibly useful feature that allows for additional analysis on a report grid using Smart View. Query-Ready Mode is discussed later in the book, but it is important to point out that you may change the settings for Query-Ready Mode in the Financial Reporting Preferences menu. The default and most common setting for Query-Ready Mode is **Smart View**. The Excel grid setting is another feature used if Smart View is not installed in the environment.

User preferences may be configured and changed at any time throughout the life of the user account.

Running a Financial Report

"So, you explained the basic features of Workspace, now what do I do from here?" There are many features that may be invoked when running a financial report. This section provides a basic understanding of executing a financial report from Workspace and touches on advanced topics discussed in later chapters to include Books, Batches, and integration with Microsoft Office.

Executing a Report in HTML & PDF Displays

Running a Financial Report from Workspace is a very simple operation. After navigating to the folder that contains the report, the Financial Report can be double-clicked to invoke the output preference set by the user in the Financial Reporting preferences, or it can be right-clicked to provide additional options for executing the report in **HTML Preview, PDF Preview**, or **Studio Preview.** The following screenshot shows the options for opening a report from the right-click menu.

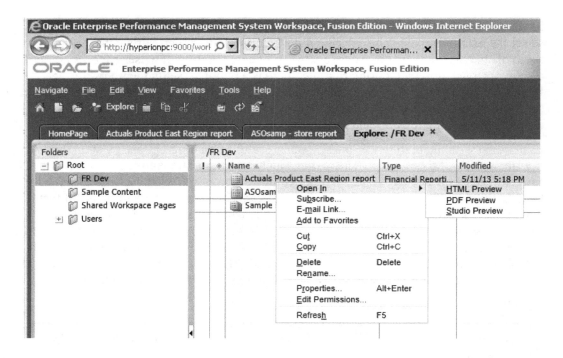

Notice the new option for opening a report in **Studio Preview**. This new feature allows a user to open a report directly into Financial Reporting Studio from Workspace for editing (provided the Studio is installed on the user's local machine).

Books and Batches

Running a report from Workspace is a pretty simple operation, but running a number of reports individually to support a collection of report outputs is a time intensive process. New users to Financial Reporting commonly ask, "Is there an automated method to build briefing books with multiple reports, various parameters, and external content?" There are two very commonly used and effective features in Financial Reporting for running sets of reports.

The first feature is a **Book,** which allows users to compile a set of reports with various parameters and external content into a single reporting package. Upon the execution of the book, the system runs all of the reports with the parameters specified and users are presented with a book output file containing all of the executed reports together in the order created by the user. The book feature is very powerful and it allows users to generate repetitive reporting content easily and seamlessly using a set of report templates.

Another important feature of Financial Reporting is the ability to run **Batches**. A batch is a scheduled job that runs a report or book on a desired schedule. Batches are typically run with a parameter file, allowing the system to run and automatically generate report output. Batch output can be saved into a directory of Workspace, e-mailed, printed, and/or saved on a local network drive. The chapters on Books, Batches, and Smart View integration provide an in-depth view into configuring and executing advanced report generation features.

Smart View Integration (Query Ready & Office Importing)

Since Smart View plays a major role in nearly all Oracle EPM applications, it is important to point out two major features of Smart View that are discussed in detail in Chapter 12. We are commonly asked, "I have a report that shows me great information but it is at summary level. How do I drill into this report?" Financial Reporting contains a feature that allows users to export the report in **Query-Ready Mode**. Query-Ready mode launches Microsoft Excel and maps the content from the HTML Financial Report to Excel. When accessed from the HTML view of the report, it even connects Smart View to the appropriate data source and then refreshes the content. The final result is an active spreadsheet allowing users to drill-down and analyze the grid content in a dynamic format.

Oracle Smart View also provides the ability to explore the contents of Workspace and import Financial Reporting components into a Microsoft Office (Excel, Word, or PowerPoint) document. Smart View maps the report content in the Office documents back to the repository, allowing the user to refresh the content in the document seamlessly. The Office integration feature is improved in the new versions of Smart View and is described in detail in Chapter 12 on Smart View Integration.

Financial Reporting Studio

The Oracle Financial Reporting Studio is a desktop-based application used to create all Financial Reports. The Studio utility, similar to the Oracle Hyperion Interactive Reporting Studio, provides a graphical drag-and-drop interface utilized to configure the features for building, generating, and calculating content displayed on a report. The application is commonly reserved for the developer community. However, releasing the developer Studio to the power-user community may benefit an organization and its development and administration teams.

What If I Do Not Have Access to FR Studio?

Most users do not have access to the Financial Reporting Studio product. Despite the fact that this is common across many environments, the expansion of the use of the Studio would serve most environments well. The goal of this book is to provide as much information as possible to bring a comfort level to users who want to build reports, and Oracle has made accessing the Studio product much easier than in the past through deploying the installation files via Workspace.

While many business environments invoke a strong software development lifecycle to ensure development quality, we have seen that educating users with knowledge of the product and including users as part of the overall development process cuts down rework, scope change, and positively impacts the development timeframe.

Installing Reporting Studio

The installation file and method of installation for the Financial Reporting Studio have changed across the different software versions - from System 9 through Oracle EPM 11.1.2.4. A new standalone executable for the Financial Reporting Studio is delivered with the client installer download. Workspace now provides the ability to install the Financial Reporting Studio through the Tools → Install menu. The following screenshot shows the installation link from Workspace:

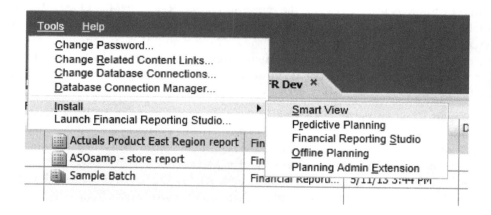

Upon clicking the Financial Reporting Studio link, a window opens displaying a download bar and a menu appears for installing the Studio. The file may be run from the menu or saved locally and then executed to start the installation.

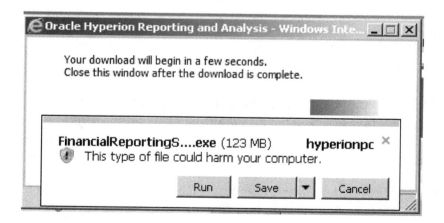

Upon executing the installation file, for version 11.1.2.3, the language selection window appears for the installation.

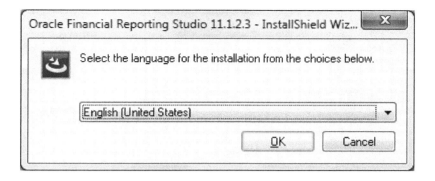

Pressing the OK button starts the install in the desired language. The installation files are extracted by the machine and the welcome screen is shown:

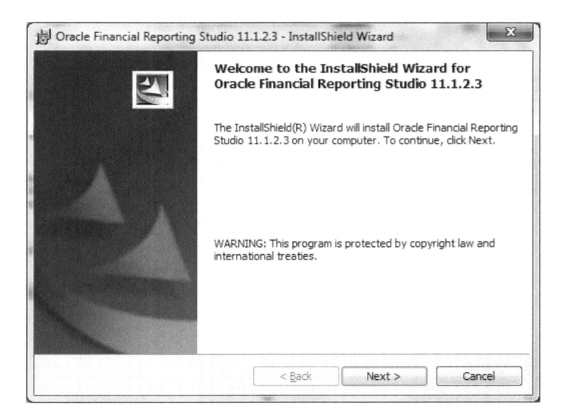

Upon pressing the Next button, the following screen allows for the selection of the destination folder for the installation:

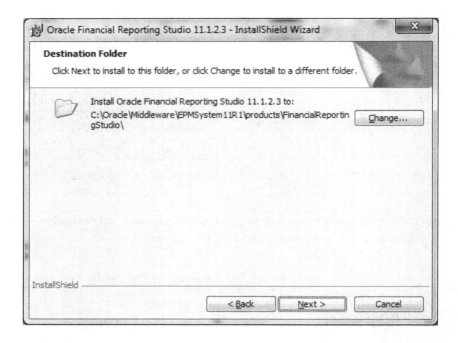

After pressing Next, a window appears for starting the installation:

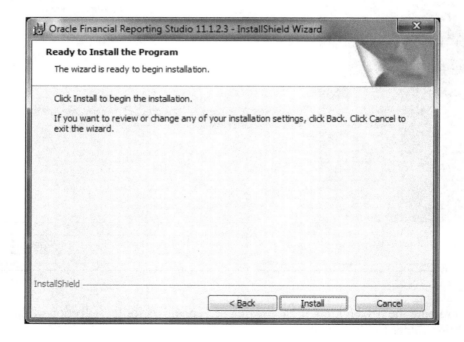

Upon pressing Install, the installer executes:

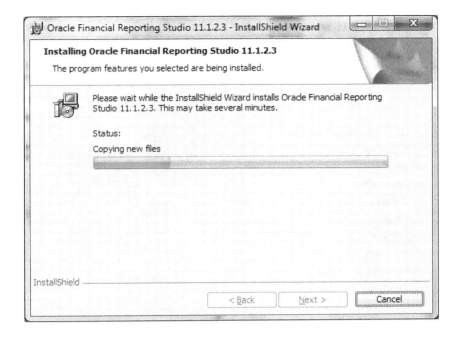

When the installation is complete, the completed window appears:

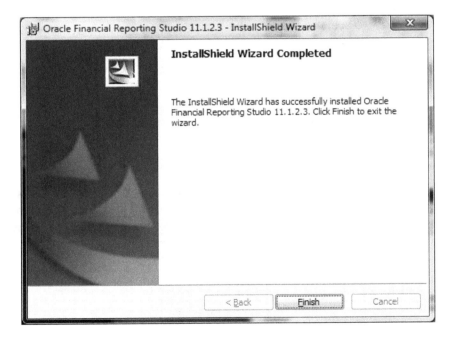

Pressing Finish completes the installation.

Logging into Financial Reporting Studio

Once the software is installed, the Studio shortcut is located in the Start → Programs menu under the Oracle → Financial Reporting Studio 11.1.2.3 folder – as shown in the following screenshot.

Selecting the Financial Reporting Studio 11.1.2.3 icon opens the Financial Reporting Studio window for authentication. Logging into the Financial Reporting Studio requires access to create reports. Users must enter their User Name and Password, and the Server URL into the login boxes – as shown in the following screenshot.

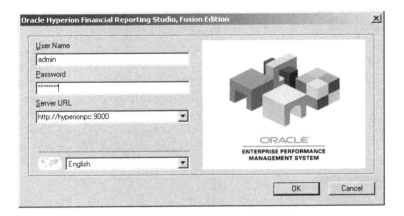

Notice that the URL contains both the prefix http:// as well as the colon (:) and port number at the end of the URL. If the URL is not exactly correct, the Studio displays an error message.

> The installation of Oracle EPM for this book was completed with the compact installation where all services are accessed across port 9000. Most enterprise deployments have Financial Reporting running on port 8200. Check with your system administration team for the appropriate URL for Oracle Financial Reporting.

Hyperion Shared Services and Access to Financial Reporting Studio

Hyperion Shared Services controls access to the application and the roles that each user or group can perform inside each application. Roles are native to Oracle EPM, and each role has a different definition of access and functionality. While it is not important to address all the different roles across all applications in this section of the book, it is important to note that the report developers need to have the **Report Designer** role, at a minimum, to access the Financial Reporting Studio product. Other key roles for Financial Reporting include the following parent roles: **Content Manager**, **Job Manager**, and **Schedule Manager**. Each parent role provides a set of features to support each activity from creating and managing content, creating jobs, and working with the built-in job scheduler. Inside each section is a set of features that can individually be applied to specific users requiring less functionality or permissions. Examples include **Data Source Publisher** for creating a Financial Reporting Data Source, the **Explorer** role for accessing the Explorer, and **Job Runner** for running scheduled jobs.

Summary

Oracle Hyperion Financial Reporting software is the current reporting engine that is used to satisfy a set of analytic and reporting requirements when working with Oracle EPM products. The chapter started with an overview of the Oracle Hyperion Financial Reporting product and the new features including the release of the product with OBIEE 11.1.1.7 as well as the new support for mobile devices. The chapter continued with an overview of the EPM Workspace, providing information on accessing and exploring content in the interface. The chapter provided insight into multiple report output options from running reports inside Workspace as well as the concepts of Books, Batches, and Smart View integration.

The chapter transitioned to information on the Financial Reporting Studio product, which is used to build and manage reports. Instructions for installing the studio were provided along with information on logging into the product, and setting the stage for building content using the software. The chapter concluded with a brief overview of the Oracle EPM roles that are assignable to the user community. Chapter 2 picks up from where Chapter 1 left off, diving further into the Financial Reporting Studio software product.

2

Working with Financial Reporting Studio & Database Connections

Financial Reports are created through the use of the Financial Reporting Studio software product with connections to applications through the use of database connection files. The Studio connects directly to the server, providing the ability to browse the report catalogue as well as create and modify reports directly in the system. Reporting objects can be developed and modified easily, and report migrations are easily completed using the export and import features. While the software was viewed as more of a developer product in past versions, it is our recommendation to open Financial Reporting development to qualified users to improve delivery capability. This chapter provides an overview of the Studio product, features, and interface, as well as setting up Financial Reporting Database Connections for connecting the reports to Oracle EPM products.

The following topics are introduced in this chapter:

- Financial Reporting Studio Interface
- Workspace Importing and Exporting
- Managing Database Connections

Financial Reporting Studio Interface

After logging into the Financial Reporting Studio, the interface displays a blank screen with the **Financial Reporting Studio Menu** and the **Standard Toolbar** as shown in the following screenshot.

From the initial interface, two main operations can be performed: create a new blank report or open an existing report. The Studio maintains an active connection to Workspace, where reports are accessed, edited, and saved directly into the system. There is no method to save a Financial Report to the local machine from the Financial Reporting Studio. Reports are moved to the local machine and saved offline through a method of exporting and importing from Workspace, which is described later in this chapter.

Creating a Report

Financial Reporting Studio connects directly to the EPM system during login and uses the file structure displayed in the EPM Workspace Explorer. Creating a new report is completed by clicking on the File → New →Report menu item of the File menu as shown in the screenshot below or through the new Report shortcut button on the toolbar.

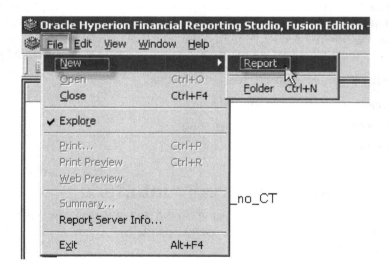

Once a selection is made by the user to create a new report, the Studio opens to a blank report development screen.

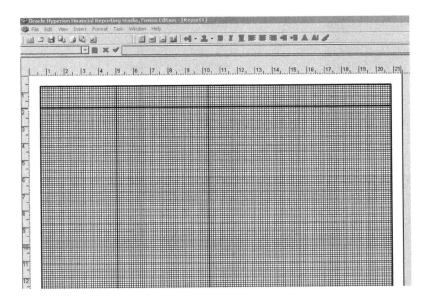

Upon initial creation, the only configurable items on the report are the header and footer height as well as the page sizing. Headers and footers are commonly used to display images, titles, runtime variable selections as well as page numbers, file names and locations, runtimes, and run-users. The **Properties Sidebar** is displayed at the right of the screen throughout the report development process. The window displays configuration options based on the selected object in the report, and it allows for the addition of a report description as well as sizing for the header and the footer. The following screenshot shows the sidebar displaying the properties for the new report.

Report Toolbars

The Financial Reporting Studio contains two main toolbars containing shortcuts for editing reports. The following is an overview of the Standard and Designer toolbars.

Standard Toolbar

The **Standard Toolbar** is displayed throughout the use of the product and contains the ability to perform functions from opening and saving the report to printing and previewing. The following screenshot displays the buttons of the toolbar.

Seven shortcuts exist on the standard toolbar. The following list details all of the options from left to right.

- **New Report** - The New Report button creates a blank report in the Financial Reporting Studio.
- **Open** - The Open button opens a window to browse the Oracle EPM Workspace file system and open an existing Financial Report.
- **Save** - The Save button saves the report in its current state. If the report has not been saved previously, a window appears to save the report in a desired location with a desired name.
- **Explore** - The Explore button brings up the Explore feature of the Hyperion EPM system, allowing a user to navigate the file system and open items that exist in the repository.
- **Print** - The Print button opens the print dialog allowing for printing and the configuration of print settings.
- **Print Preview** - The Print preview button displays the report as it would appear when printed. It is important to test both PDF and HTML printing before feeling comfortable with the display of the report as formatting may vary between outputs.
- **Web Preview** - The Web Preview button shows a preview of the report run in HTML format. HTML preview should be accompanied by a PDF format test to thoroughly test reporting output.

Designer Toolbar

The **Designer Toolbar** contains a set of shortcuts commonly used when building a report. The shortcuts cover building a grid through text and layout formatting. The following screenshot displays the toolbar.

Seventeen shortcuts exist on the toolbar. The following descriptions highlight each feature from left to right.

- **Insert Grid** - The Insert Grid button is used to create a new grid, configured by drawing the grid into the working area of the report.
- **Insert Text** - The Insert Text button is used to insert a text box into the report. Text boxes are commonly used for labels, notes, headers, and footers.
- **Insert Image** - The Insert Image button is used to insert an image into the report. Images are commonly used to support logos and other custom imagery.
- **Insert Chart** - The Insert Chart button is used to insert a chart object into the report. Charts require grids and read data from a grid for the chart display.
- **Insert Row** - The Insert Row button inserts a row *above* a highlighted row in a grid.
- **Insert Column** - The Insert Column button inserts a column to the *left* of a highlighted column in a grid.
- **Bold**, **Italic**, and **Underline** - These buttons apply bold, italic, and underline features respectively.
- **Left**, **Center**, and **Right Justify** - These buttons align selected text to the left, center, and right respectively.
- **Increase** and **Decrease Indent** - The Increase Indent button increases the indent of the selected text, and the Decrease Indent button decreases the indent of the selected text.
- **Format** - The Format button opens the Format Cells dialog box, containing a set of formatting options.
- **Conditional Format** - The Conditional Format button opens the Conditional Format dialog box, which is used to configure conditional formatting to the sections highlighted in the report. Conditional Formatting is a very powerful feature in Financial Reporting and is applied in certain criteria to show different formatting based on values displayed.
- **Format Painter** - The Format Painter button applies the format of a selected cell or cell range to a target cell or cell range. The Format Painter is a very powerful feature that aids in performing rapid format changes.

Adding Content through Reporting Objects

Four main Financial Reporting objects are used to generate report content: Grid, Chart, Text Labels, and Image. The objects are added from the Insert menu or through their respective icons on the Designer toolbar. The following sections provide an overview of each object.

Grid

The **Grid** is the foundation for data in a report. Grid objects make connections to Essbase, Hyperion Planning, or Hyperion Financial Management data sources and provide significant functionality for querying, displaying, and integrating content. Multiple grids can be used in a single report, and data from one or more grids can be joined together to display data across multiple applications.

Chart

A **Chart** object links to a grid and displays a graphical depiction of the information in the grid. Charts provide three main formatting options (Bar, Line, and Pie) and a combination option to display both a bar and a line. The charts are not comparable to the features of Microsoft Excel charts, but charts still provide a solid approach for graphically displaying data especially when used in concert with Books and Batches, a method to run multiple scenarios from one reporting template.

Text Labels

Text Labels provide static and dynamic content in reports. Text labels are commonly used in headers, footers, and occasionally in the report body. Text labels may be heavily formatted and may contain typed information as well as Financial Reporting functions to display dynamic content.

Images

Image objects allow for pictures to be added to the document. Images are commonly used to display logos and can be stretched and positioned across any section of the report. At this time, only .jpg, .gif, and .bmp image file formats are allowed.

Saving Files

Saving and saving often is a key component for success with Financial Reporting Studio. Since the connection between Studio and the file system is typically across the corporate network, it is important to save the report multiple times. If the services go down or if the network falters, having the report saved close to its current state ensures the report development is not lost.

> If access is lost to the server, keep the report open and try to resave when the system is back online. In most cases the Studio is able to recover when access to the system is brought back online.

When working with a report and testing different features and settings, it is important to save backup copies of reports during the development process. This provides the ability to return to key checkpoints in the development process without needing to scrap and recreate the report. Typically, report developers have multiple versions of a report when developing, allowing for analysis and the testing of functionality without having to recreate the report if a development approach does not produce desirable results.

A report is saved by pressing the Save button on the toolbar or through the Save option on the File menu. After pressing Save for the first time or when pressing Save As, the following window appears allowing for the ability to save the report in a desired folder with a desired name.

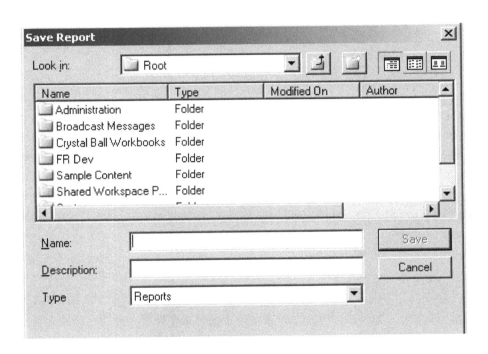

Exporting and Importing from Workspace

In addition to saving multiple versions, report developers can take a backup of reports from Workspace. The Export feature is commonly used to export reports from one environment and import them into another environment, but it can also be used to back-up copies of reports for offline storage. The feature also provides an extra benefit through its ability to export multiple reports at a time.

Exporting reports from Workspace is completed by selecting Export from the File menu while in the Explore window of Workspace as shown in the following screenshot.

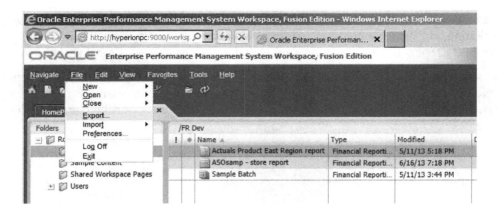

Upon selecting Export, the Select Financial Reporting Documents to Export window appears. The export can contain one or many reports from a single folder as well as any part of the folder structure in Workspace. Therefore, the entire set of reports from the system can be exported from the Root directory (if desired). The following screenshot displays the selection of two reports for export.

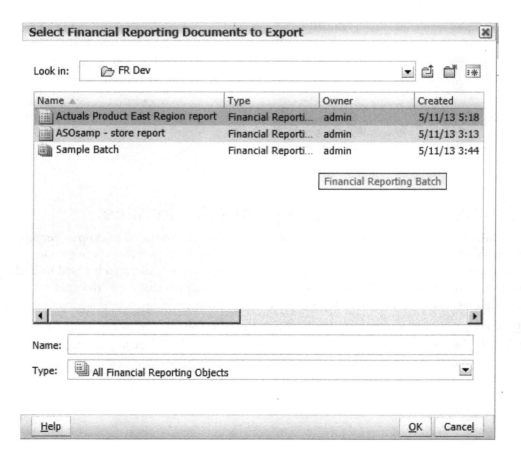

Upon selecting OK, the system prepares the files for export and displays the following message.

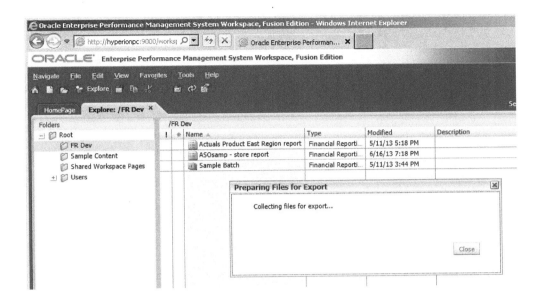

When complete, a dialogue box appears within the browser that asks for the next steps with the file created. The system exports the file into a standard extension based on the financial reporting object for single files, and the system creates a zip file for multiple objects and folders.

Selecting Save As opens the dialogue box for the save location as shown in the following screenshot.

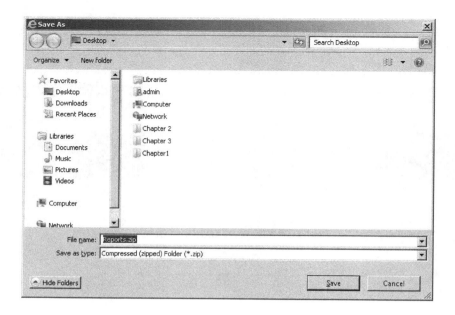

Opening the zip file displays the exported reports and folder structure as shown below.

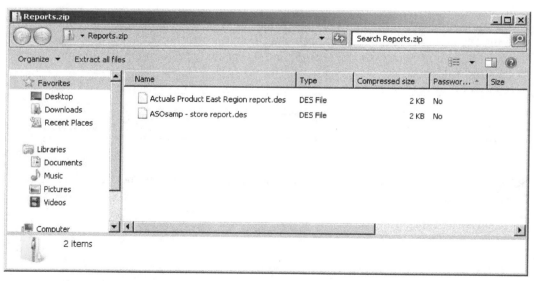

Notice the individual Report objects exported from the system contain the extension
`.des`.

Importing Exported Reports into Workspace

Reports are easily imported into the system in any folder of Workspace. When a report
export is imported into Workspace, the entire exported content is imported into the active

folder. All folders in the export are created in Workspace and the report content is added into the system.

Importing Financial Reporting objects into the system is completed through selecting Import → Financial Reporting Documents as shown in the following screenshot.

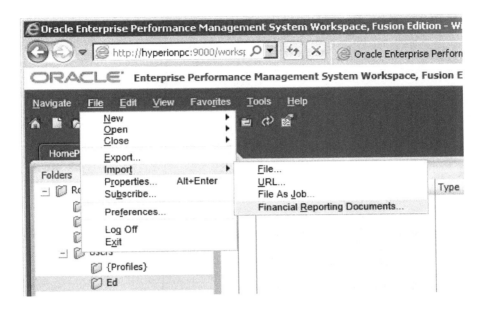

Upon selecting the Import option, a window appears as per the following screenshot.

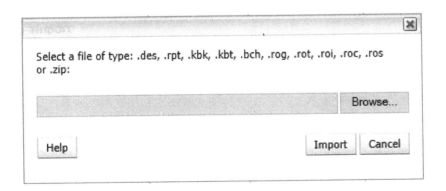

Multiple Financial Reporting object formats may be imported along with the .zip file format that is created when multiple objects are exported. In the following example, the two reports previously exported are reimported into the Users → Ed folder within Workspace.

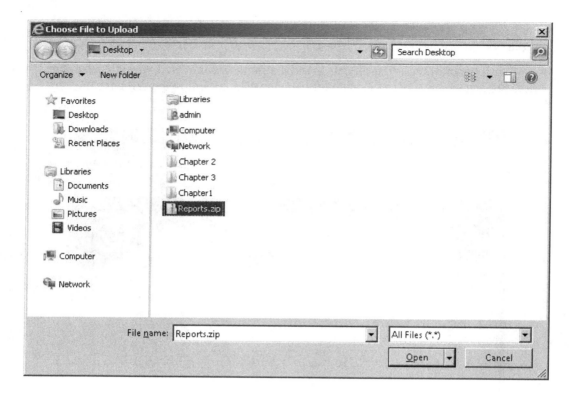

If a file already exists inside the folder with the same name and file path, a warning message appears asking to overwrite, skip (no), or cancel the import as shown in the following screenshot.

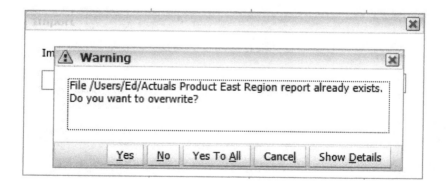

Selecting one of the yes options completes the import and the updated reports and folders show inside the imported folder.

Database Connections

Adding data to a Financial Report with active content from a Hyperion Planning, Essbase, or Hyperion Financial Management (HFM) application requires the creation of a **Database Connection**. A database connection establishes connections into the different Hyperion applications and brokers the transfer of content from the application to Financial Reporting. The database connection files are specific to an individual application or cube. Connections are assigned to grid objects in each report, and multiple connections may be leveraged in a single report.

Creating a Database Connection

The database connections for Financial Reporting are not created in the Financial Reporting Studio, but rather through specific utilities in Workspace. The creation of database connections are typically limited to Hyperion Reporting Administrators, and creating the database connection in Hyperion requires the **Database Connection Manager** role or higher level privileges in Hyperion Shared Services for the user account creating the database connections.

Creating a database connection from Workspace is accomplished by logging into Workspace with a user account provisioned appropriately and navigating to Explore. From the Explore section, the Tools menu is accessed and the Database Connection Manager is selected as shown in the following screenshot.

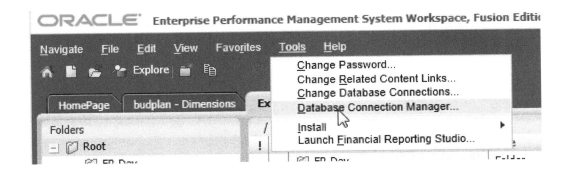

The **Database Connection Manager** is the location where all of the database connections for Financial Reporting are stored for the deployment. New connections are created in this utility and existing connections may be modified.

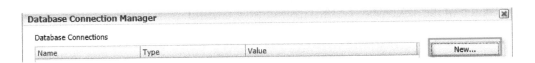

Pressing the New button brings up the Database Connection Properties window as shown in the following screenshot.

Database Connection Properties contains a set of configuration items necessary to create an active connection to one of the Hyperion applications. The example above depicts connecting to an Oracle Essbase application and database. Notice the connection contains a Name field for labeling the connection string. There is also a Type field for the selection of Essbase, Planning, or Financial Management (HFM). In the Essbase example, there is a field for the Server as well as authentication information and the Application and Database for the selection of the specific cube.

The connection for Hyperion Financial Management is created by using the Type FinancialManagement. Once the Server and credentials are set, the Application is selected using the application selection button shown next to the text box for the Application in the screenshot below.

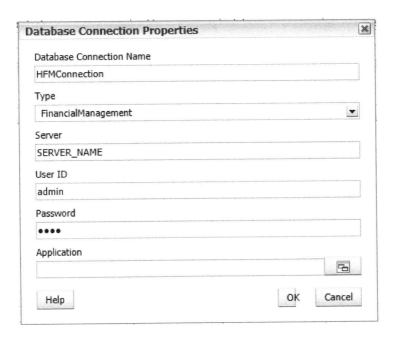

The connection for Hyperion Planning is similar to the Essbase and Financial Management connections but requires the Application and Database name to be typed into the Connection Properties window instead of through a selection. A Hyperion Planning connection is created by using the type Planning with the configuration demonstrated below.

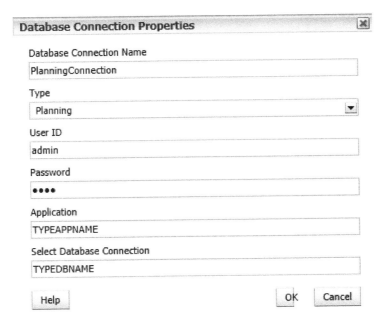

Editing a Database Connection

Editing a database connection is completed in a similar fashion to creating a new connection. Editing a database connection is important, especially when a set of existing reports need to point to a new database. These circumstances commonly occur at the rollover of the fiscal year or other specific time period, when the standard report templates are changed over to a new application. A database connection is changed by opening the **Database Connection Manager**, selecting the connection of interest, and selecting Edit. The existing settings appear in the Database Connection Properties window similar to creating a new database connection. The database connection is updated by pressing the OK button after making the desired changes.

Switching the Database Connections in a Report

EPM Workspace contains an additional utility used to switch the database connections in a report. The **Change Database Connections** utility allows for the changing of one or more connections in a report, which is very commonly used when a set of reports require a database connection change to a new connection file. This approach is also commonly used when a copy of a report is made and the connection strings are changed to point to different Oracle EPM applications. This feature is similar to changing the database connection itself, but allows for an individual report to be changed without impacting the other reports using the same database connection.

Changing the database connection for a report begins with the selection of the Change Database Connections menu item from the Tools menu in the Explore section of Workspace. Upon selecting the Change Database Connections menu item, the following window appears for the selection of the report to change.

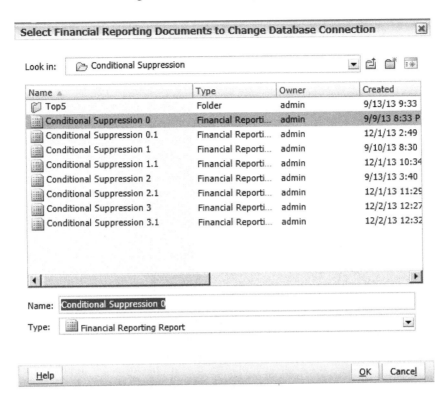

After navigating to the report of interest, selecting OK opens the Change Database Connection menu as shown in the following screenshot.

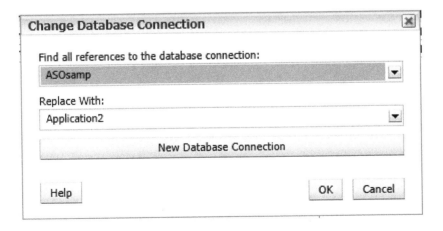

All of the database connections in the report appear in the first drop-down, and the list of available connection options appear in the second drop-down. Making the selections and pressing the OK button makes the connection change, and the system displays a success or failure message.

> The system does not check to see if the database connection results in the successful execution of the report. It is important to check the report after the database connection change to make sure it workes properly. It would also be worthwhile to take an export or copy of the reports before making changes to the live copy to ensure no issues exist after the change.

Summary

Understanding the features of the Financial Reporting Studio and the interface to create and manage database connections are the first steps toward creating a report in the application. While the chapter was primarily administrative, an understanding of the Financial Reporting Studio and reporting object management plays an important role in report development and maintenance. The focus of this chapter was to provide an overview of the Financial Reporting Studio, the methods used to create a database connection, and report importing and exporting techniques. The chapter started with an overview of the FR Studio and shortcut features commonly used by developers. The methods to create a new report were demonstrated and the methods for saving a report into Workspace were displayed. The chapter continued into an overview of exporting and importing reports from Workspace to demonstrate the capabilities of saving content offline and migrating content between environments. Finally, the chapter concluded with steps to create and manage report database connections, which segues into the next chapter which demonstrates the steps for adding content to reports through the use of grids.

3

Grids: Basic Operations, Charting, and the Point of View

Grids are the core element of a financial report and provide a means of querying and displaying data from various data sources. Many different approaches and variations of grids may exist in a financial report, providing the framework to support analysis, data discovery, and analytics. This chapter provides an overview of grids and the basic grid functionality that exists within the Financial Reporting software. Later chapters dig further into grids, showing advanced formatting, formulas, and suppression techniques.

The following content is introduced in this chapter:

- Building a Grid
- Grid Options
- Basic Member Selection & Grid Display
- The Point of View
- Charting

What is a Grid?

A **Grid** is a Financial Reporting object that queries and displays data from an Essbase, Hyperion Planning, or Hyperion Financial Management application. Grids leverage database connections to connect to various sources and use an Oracle proprietary method for querying data from the applications. The data returned from a grid is displayed in a columnar format (rows and columns) and may be manipulated using a large variety of grid options. Simple reports may contain only one grid pulling from a single data source. More complicated reports may contain multiple grids with one or more data sources in each grid.

Building a Grid

Adding data to the report from an Essbase, Hyperion Planning, or Hyperion Financial Management application requires the creation of a grid object inside the report. A grid makes a connection to the selected database and queries the source during runtime. A grid is created by selecting Insert → Grid from the File menu when editing a report.

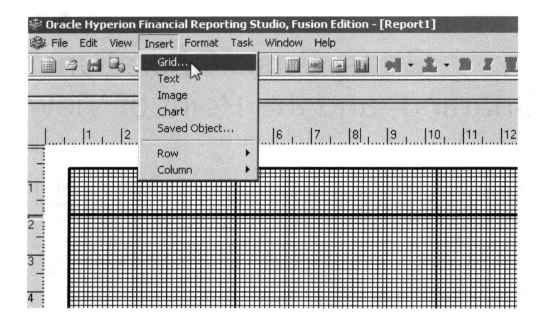

Upon selecting the Grid object, the mouse cursor changes, allowing the grid to be created in the report - by *draw*ing it in the working area.

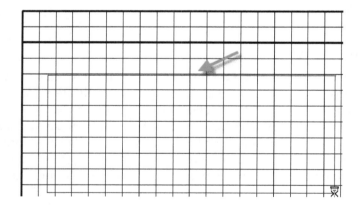

When complete, the Select a Database Connection window appears:

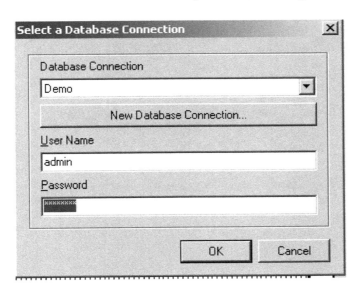

The window contains three boxes for input from the user. The first option is for selecting the database connection from a list of connections configured in Workspace. The database connection may be for Planning, Essbase, or Hyperion Financial Management. In the example screenshots used in this chapter, Essbase is the selected database connection. The second and third boxes on the screen are for authenticating the connection with the application.

Each database connection requires a specific User ID and Password with access to the application.

Once the appropriate connection is selected and the user and password entered, clicking OK brings up the Dimension Layout configuration screen as shown in the following screenshot.

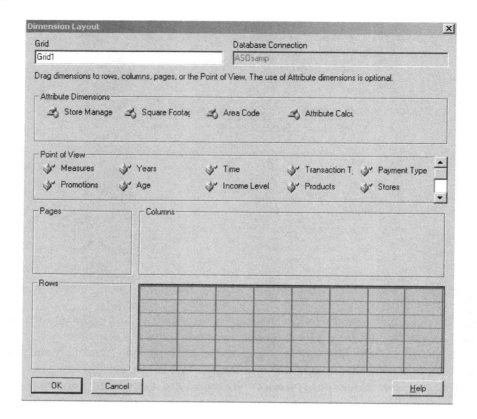

The dimension layout screen is used to create the data layout displayed when a report is run and contains different sections for configuring the layout of the grid. The top of the screen contains a box named Grid for specifying a name for the grid object. The name of the grid is used when referencing the grid throughout the report development process, and the name should be kept short and simple for ease of reference. The box in the upper right-hand portion of the screen shows the database connection selected for the grid. The other five sections of the Essbase grid are used to configure the layout of the dimensions for the grid. The four main sections are detailed as follows:

- Point of View – By default, all dimensions in the application display in the **Point of View** (excluding any attribute dimensions). The developer can decide to move the dimensions into rows, columns, pages, or leave the dimensions in the Point of View.

- Pages – The **Pages** section is used to break the report's content into separate pages by the values of the dimensions added to the page section of the dimension layout.

- Rows – The **Rows** section is used for displaying the hierarchical values of the selected dimensions in the rows of the grid.

- Columns – The **Columns** section is used for displaying the hierarchical values of the selected dimensions in the columns of the grid.

In the screenshot, notice the section for Attribute Dimensions. Attribute Dimensions are objects in Hyperion Planning and Essbase that are tagged to a dimension and optional for use in reporting. Attribute Dimensions do not appear in the Point of View section of the dimension layout by default because Attributes do not have a direct impact on the data intersection but rather serve as another method of segmentation. If there is an interest in using Attribute Dimensions in an application, attributes may be dragged into the Point of View, pages, rows, or columns.

Example Grid Configuration

The following example highlights a simple case of configuring a grid using an Essbase database connection. On the data layout screen, the Time and Geography dimensions are moved into the Column section through dragging and dropping from the Point of View section and the Products dimension is moved into the Rows section.

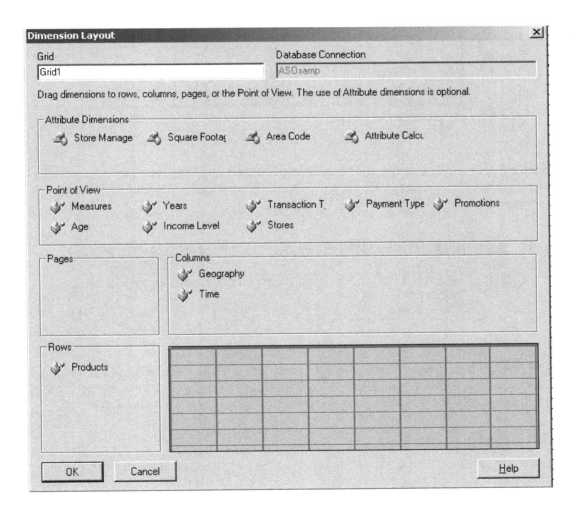

Pressing the OK button builds the grid as shown in the following screenshot.

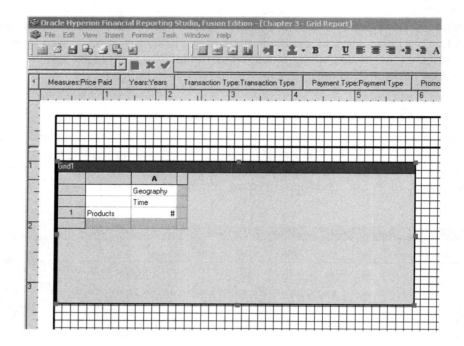

Notice that in addition to the grid there is an additional bar at the top of the screen that displays the dimensions that are set in the Point of View as shown in the following screenshot.

The Point of View serves as another filter for the report. The Point of View bar denotes the dimensions and selected values for each dimension, which defaults to the top level of the dimension. The Point of View is discussed in a later section of this chapter.

Grid Options

Grids contain many configuration options for enhancing the data displayed in the grid. The Studio interface displays a properties window on the right-hand side of the screen that shows the properties associated with the selected item in the report development window. The properties window for Grid Properties displays three sets of options including General, Suppression, and Position.

General Grid Settings

The General grid properties show by default when a grid is selected in the main report window. The following screenshot displays a list of settings for the General Grid Properties.

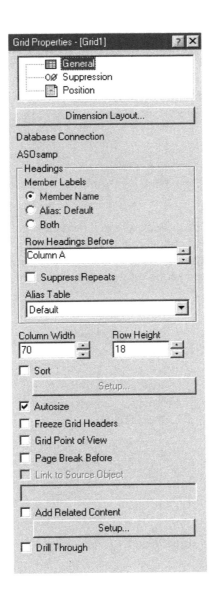

Starting from the top of the list, the Dimension Layout button is used to reopen the dimension layout window for editing the Point of View, Rows, Columns, and Pages configuration of the grid. Editing the dimension configuration modifies the grid configuration and may significantly alter the report layout based on the changes made.

Save a copy of your current report before making dimension layout changes so you can revert back if the layout changes do not work as planned.

Slightly below the dimension layout button is the name of the database connection for the grid. The database connection name is a useful label, providing information on the database connection used in the grid. As more grids are used in the report and as the environment expands, it is important to know the database connections for report troubleshooting and maintenance.

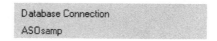

The Headings section of the properties window provides the ability to set default settings for grid headings. Any settings changed in this section apply across the entire grid. Similar settings exist while editing rows, columns, and even cells. Applying heading formatting with a more defined scope may provide easier maintenance when working with grid labels.

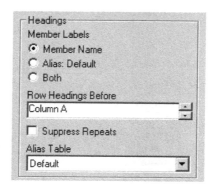

The following is an overview of the Headings features:

- Member Labels – The Member Labels section allows for the configuration of label settings for the entire grid. Selecting **Member Name** or **Alias** shows either the name, or alias respectively, for the displayed grid's dimension members. Selecting **Both** shows the member name and then the alias next to the name in the column.

- Row Headings Before – The **Row Headings Before** feature is a very powerful part of Financial Reporting. It allows for the movement of row headings into the middle of the grid. This approach allows the developer to split the data values to the left and right of the grid headings. Booklet reports are created using this feature by setting the row headings in the center of the report and showing data on either side. Setting this value is completed by selecting the column location to display the row headings.

- Suppress Repeats – The **Suppress Repeats** option impacts both the rows and the columns of the grid and suppresses repeated headings in both columns and rows. The setting can also be applied, under a more narrow scope, to individual rows and columns.

- Alias Table – This feature is used to set the Alias Table when displaying aliases in the grid. If only one Alias Table exists, the **Default** alias table is used.

After the headings section of the properties window, there are settings for the default Column Width and Row Height and a checkbox for configuring sorting. Clicking the Sort checkbox activates the Setup button. Upon launching the Setup button, a window displaying sorting options similar to those in Microsoft Excel appears.

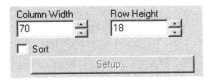

Below the Sort checkbox, four other checkboxes appear allowing for the configuration of additional grid properties. One of the most important settings is the Grid Point of View.

| ☑ Autosize |
| ☐ Freeze Grid Headers |
| ☐ Grid Point of View |
| ☐ Page Break Before |

Turning on the Grid Point of View displays the Point of View for the grid *in the grid itself.* This feature makes it easier to see the Point of View configuration for each grid, and the setting allows for the configuration of grid-specific Point of View selections. The following screenshot shows the Grid Point of View turned on.

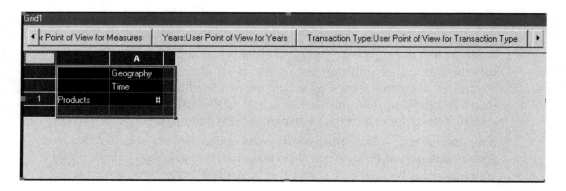

Note: You may need to expand the grid slightly to get a better view of the Grid Point of View.

The following is a description of the other three checkboxes.

- Autosize – The **Autosize** option is turned on by default and keeping this setting checked allows Financial Reporting to automatically resize a grid as necessary.

- Freeze Grid Headers – The **Freeze Grid Headers** option provides the ability to freeze the headers of the grid when scrolling.

- Page Break Before – The **Page Break Before** option allows the user to have the report insert a page break before the grid is displayed. Configuring the layout of multiple grids with page breaks can be complicated. It may require some trial-and-error with spacing the grids and even creating blank space at the bottom of the grids to display them in the desired format on the page.

The last three options in the properties window are Link to Source Object, Adding Related Content, and Drill Through. These features are useful for integrating the grid with source data, other Hyperion objects, and linked objects.

Row, Column, and Cell Properties

In addition to general grid properties, there are also a set of Row, Column, and Cell properties. The following screenshot shows the Column Properties window with Column A in the report selected.

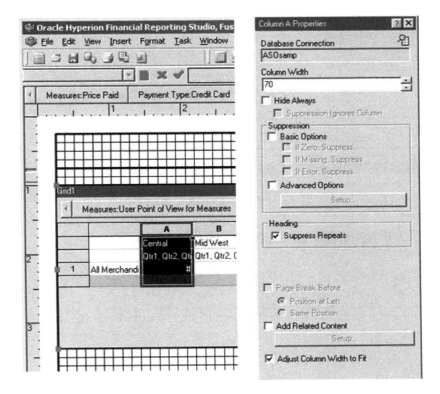

Notice the designation of Column A in the properties window, above, which allows for the setting of individual column properties. The column properties window contains the ability to modify a column's sizing settings, suppression settings, and the ability to add related content. A very common feature that is used in column settings is the Hide Always setting, which hides the column from display. This allows for columns to be used in report functions without the need to display column values at runtime. The Adjust Column Width-to-Fit setting is useful for formatting and allows for an auto adjustment of the column width to the width of the largest value in the column.

Row Properties are similar to column properties but contain a few slight differences. The following is a screenshot of a report open to the row properties with Row 1 selected.

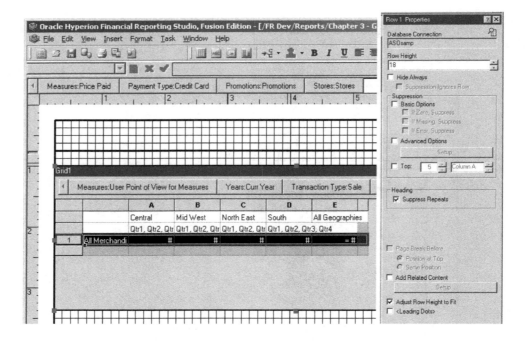

Notice the designation of Row 1 in the properties window label. Similar to columns, each row may contain a separate set of properties. The row properties window contains the ability to modify row sizing settings, suppression settings, and the ability to add related content. The Hide Always setting also exists for the row, allowing for the hiding of the row from display but still allowing for its use. One additional setting of row properties that does not exist in column properties is the Top Suppression setting. This is used to display only a subset of rows dependent upon a set of ranking criteria.

Cell options vary, depending on whether the type of cell selected is *Data*, *Formula*, or *Text*. They are commonly used to override row or column options. Cell options are identified when a specific cell is selected in the report.

Suppression Grid Settings

Suppression settings provide a way to hide a particular set of data across the entire grid, provide text replacement options, and a means to hide the grid. The following screenshot shows the Suppression options for a grid.

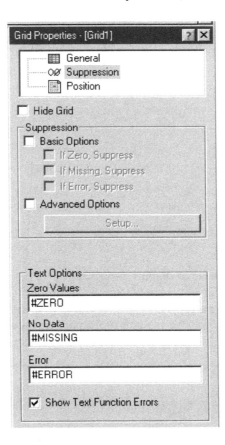

Basic suppression and conditional suppression, used to hide data based on conditions, is discussed in detail in Chapter 7.

Hiding the Grid

The first option on the options toolbar is the Hide Grid setting, which is used to remove the grid from display during runtime. The Hide Grid setting is commonly used with reports showing only charts or reports that have grids that are used to supply data to another grid (and are not shown in the report at runtime).

Text Options (Cell Replacement)

Text Options are a set of text boxes for replacing each one of the *Zero*, *No Data* (Missing), or *Error* values that may be experienced when running a report. When a report is run, the report displays the text associated with each value if any of the three values are experienced. The screenshot below shows a report that has been run with the default text option settings.

Years: Years Time: Time Transaction Type: Sale Income Level: Income Level Stores: Stores Geography: Geography			
	Original Price	Price Paid	Variance
Digital Cameras	1,275,216	1,267,367	7,849
Camcorders	2,606,617	2,591,322	15,295
Photo Printers	1,246,060	1,238,122	7,938
Digital Cameras/Camcorders	5,127,893	5,096,812	31,081
Handhelds	#MISSING	#MISSING	#ERROR
Memory	2,455,370	2,437,885	17,485
Other Accessories	6,078,599	6,038,558	40,041
Handhelds/PDAs	8,533,969	8,476,443	57,526

Notice the Handhelds row of data displays #MISSING for the Original Price and Price Paid values as well as #ERROR for the Variance column. The error is due to the Variance column containing a formula that is not able to create a division of two non-existent (missing) values. Updating the cell replacement values to some other value displays the replaced value in the report. The following screenshot shows setting the replacement values to 0.

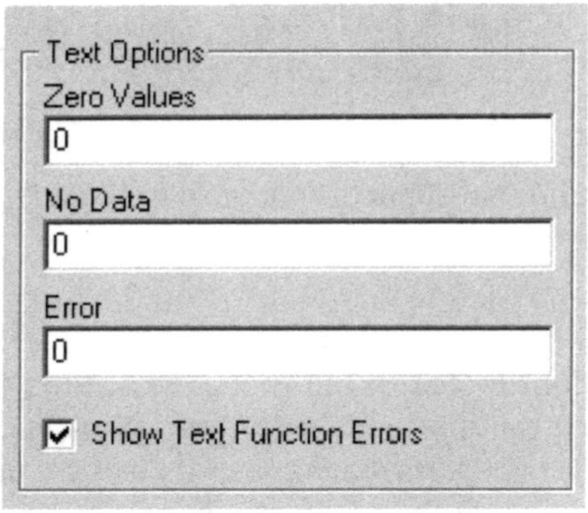

Text Options
Zero Values
0
No Data
0
Error
0
☑ Show Text Function Errors

Running the report with the 0 replacement values displays the following output.

Years: Years Time: Time Transaction Type: Sale Income Level: Income Level Stores: Stores Geography: Geography			
	Original Price	Price Paid	Variance
Digital Cameras	1,275,216	1,267,367	7,849
Camcorders	2,606,617	2,591,322	15,295
Photo Printers	1,246,060	1,238,122	7,938
Digital Cameras/Camcorders	5,127,893	5,096,812	31,081
Handhelds	0	0	0
Memory	2,455,370	2,437,885	17,485
Other Accessories	6,078,599	6,038,558	40,041
Handhelds/PDAs	8,533,969	8,476,443	57,526

Notice all of the values for the Handhelds row of data now show 0. Similarly, updating the cell replacement values to blank shows blank values, and updating to a dash (as one would expect) shows dashes. These values may be set to the preference of the user community, and can easily be changed at any time.

Position Settings

The position of a grid on a report is set by using the Position options. Position options for the grid are found by selecting the entire grid and selecting Position from the Grid Properties pane as shown in the following screenshot.

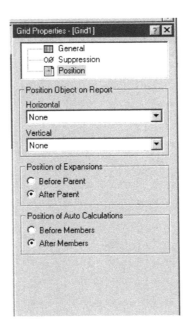

51

Position options are fairly limited and contain the ability to set the horizontal and vertical position of the grid on the report. Additionally, they provide the general settings for the position of Expansions or Auto Calculations in the report. Managing the position of multiple grids in a report can be complex and may require trial and error as well as sizing modifications to obtain effective displays.

Configuring the Grid Display (Selecting Members)

Once an initial grid is created, the next step in building a report is to build out the grid to the desired layout. The following screenshot is a continuation from the earlier example with the initial grid displayed.

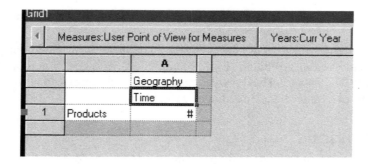

Selecting Members

Modifying members on the grids is completed by double-clicking the cell of interest, which opens the Select Members window for the grid. The following screenshot shows the Select Members window for the Time dimension.

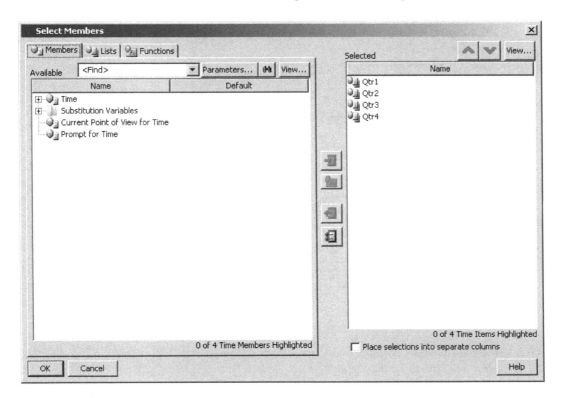

Notice that the Select Members window contains a number of settings to configure the selection of members. In the screenshot above, the member Time was removed from the selected pane, and the Time dimension was expanded. The members for the four quarters of the year were brought into the selected pane. When more than one dimension value is selected, the report displays all of the dimension values separated by commas in the designer display. The designer display with commas signifies that the column of the report will be split into separate columns during runtime.

Notice that Col A, in the screenshot below, displays the values in the second row of the header separated by commas in a single column. Also notice the change in the first row for Col A from Geography to the individual member Central. Changing the value from Geography to Central was completed in a similar fashion to changing the values from Time to Q1, Q2, Q3, Q4, but only a single member - Central - was selected.

The selection of only a single member is a common approach, allowing for complete control of the column containing a member of interest. Additional members are then added to the report through the addition of new columns.

Adding a new column to a report is completed by selecting any column or the small, non-labeled column to the far right of the report, right-clicking, selecting Insert Column, and then the data type of interest. In the example below, the Data column is used to add an additional column of data from the application. Additional options exist for adding formulas and text, which are discussed in later chapters.

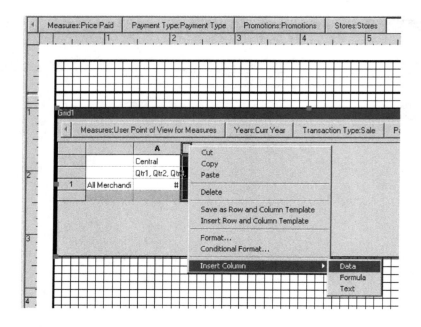

After selecting the Data column, the values from the previous column are copied into the new column, identified by the letter B.

The new Col B can be defined with a similar or completely different set of members from the Geography and Time dimension. For the sake of simplicity, the Time dimension in the column is still set to display all four quarters, and the Geography dimension has been set to display the value Mid West as shown next.

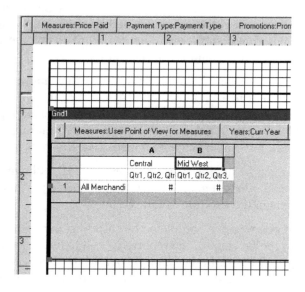

Adding a few more columns with varied Geography values, the report displays as follows.

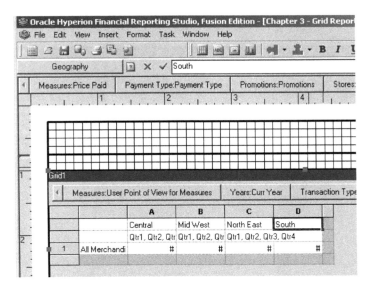

Chapter 5 continues with the example and demonstrates adding formulas and advanced member selection operations.

The Point of View

Application dimensions that are not used in grid rows, columns, or page areas need to be set to a value to display the correct intersection of data. This requirement is consistent with querying an Essbase, Hyperion Planning, or HFM application through Smart View, where the intersection of the desired data *must* be defined across all dimensions.

The Point of View is set by clicking on a dimension in the report Point of View or in the Grid Point of View. Clicking on the member (in either Point of View) brings up the following window:

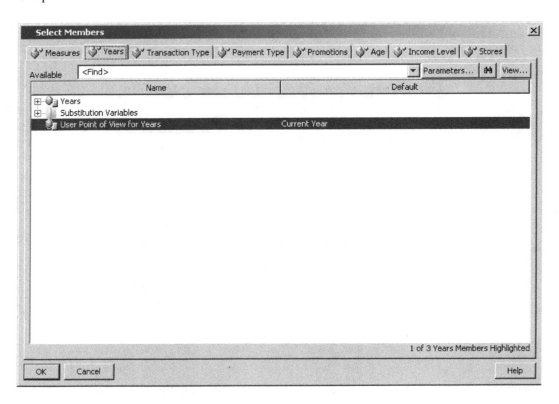

Notice that the Select Members window contains a set of tabs across the top for the different dimensions contained in the Point of View. The Point of View window allows for the selection of only one value for each dimension and the value can be only one of the following options:

- Dimension Value – The Point of View can be set to the top value of the dimension or any member in the dimension. For example, the Years dimension can be set at the top value for all years, a specific year, or any level in-between.

- Substitution Variables – Substitution Variables are dynamic variable objects that are defined in the application. These objects are changed when desired by the application owner, or automated processes, and are commonly used in reports to change report content without having to modify the report.

- User Point of View – The User Point of View setting is used to prompt the user to select the dimension value at runtime. This setting is one of the most powerful settings of the report and it is used to make the report dynamic. Effective use of the User Point of View is key to the development of dynamic reporting templates.

When working in the Grid Point of View, setting the values to a member removes the dimension from the Report Point of View. Using the Point of View effectively reduces the number of reports created through the ability to create templates allowing users to select desired values at runtime.

Charting

Charts provide the ability to reflect data pulled from a grid in a graphical format. The charting options are less friendly than the ones found in Oracle BI or Microsoft Excel, but chart objects still serve as valuable objects for tracking trends and displaying data. Charts are inserted into a report from the Insert menu, similar to adding a grid. Once the new chart is selected, the chart is inserted into the report by drawing the chart object in the report development window in the desired location. Once complete, the chart displays as follows:

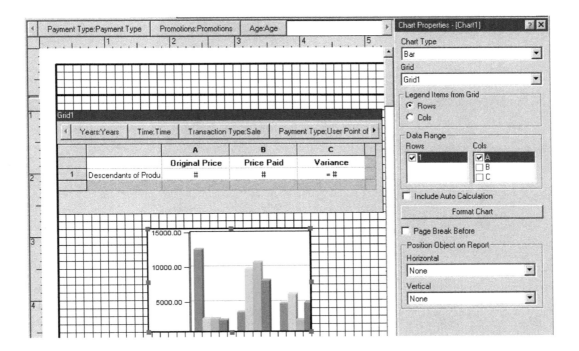

There are four types of charts available in Financial Reporting: Bar, Line, Pie, and Combo (Bar/Line). The chart object requires a grid to exist to populate the data in a chart. In the following example, the chart is changed from a bar chart to a pie chart. Additionally, the data range is updated to select Col B as well as Col A and Row 1.

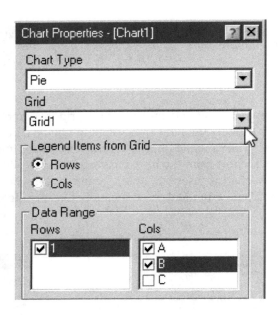

Saving and running the chart displays the following (with the grid hidden):

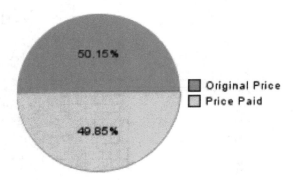

Notice the chart displays the two columns of the grid in the pie chart. Charts have limited formatting options and are configured by selecting the Format Chart button on the right of the menu. Four tabs appear with the first tab showing general Appearance settings.

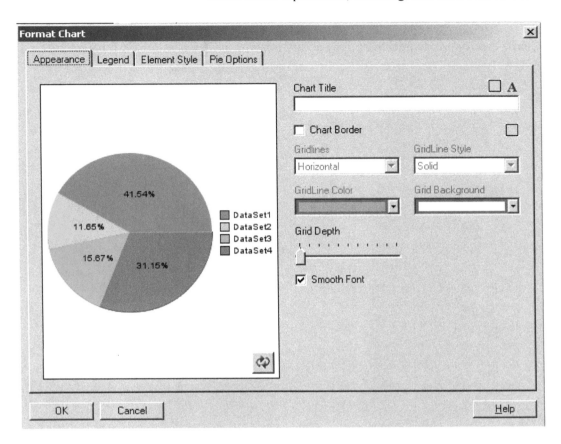

Chart titles, borders, and a few aesthetic changes may be implemented for each chart. The Legend tab is used for configuring the legend, and the Element Style configures the aesthetics for each data element. There are also tabs for each specific chart type from axis settings to specific bar, line, and pie options. Each of these options provides the ability to generate effective visual content with reports.

Summary

Grids are the core, and most complex, feature in Financial Reporting, providing the interface between reports and data sources. A majority of the functionality for a report is embedded into a grid, and grid complexity can range from a simple standard query to the introduction of logic to produce a complex deliverable. This chapter focused on introducing grid functionality and basic grid operations, and it started with adding grids to a report and configuring the dimension layout. An overview of grid options was provided, including general display settings, methods for replacing zero, missing, and error cells, hiding, and general position settings. The chapter demonstrated the configuration of the grid display, including an overview of basic member selection across report rows and columns. Subsequently, an overview of the Point of View for the report - providing information on setting both grid-level and report-level Point of View configurations - was provided. The chapter concluded with a brief overview of using Charts in a report, demonstrating the ability to show graphical output in Financial Reporting.

4

Grids: Basic Formatting

Building successful Financial Reporting deliverables requires an understanding of the different formatting options and methods available in the application. Once a grid is populated with data, many options exist for changing the aesthetic view of the data displayed in it. Oracle has provided significant flexibility with the formatting options of Financial Reporting to accommodate the many desired formatting concepts commonly seen in spreadsheet-prepared reports. This chapter describes the basic formatting options and demonstrates how to format a sample grid.

The following content is introduced in this chapter:

- Grid Formatting Options
- Grid Formatting Example

Grid Formatting Options

Grids can be formatted across their entirety or down to the row, column, or even the individual cell itself. A grid is formatted by selecting the section in the grid of interest and then selecting Format from the right-click menu or Format → Cells from the menu as shown in the following screenshot.

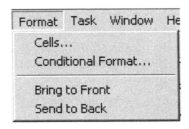

Notice the option for selecting Conditional Format from the Format menu. Conditional Formatting is the method used to apply formatting based on a set of conditional logic and is a very powerful feature of the product. Conditional Formatting is discussed, in detail, in Chapter 6, *Conditional Formatting*.

Number Formatting

The first tab in the format window displays **Number** formatting options, which provides the ability to alter the format of the numeric values for selected cells in a grid.

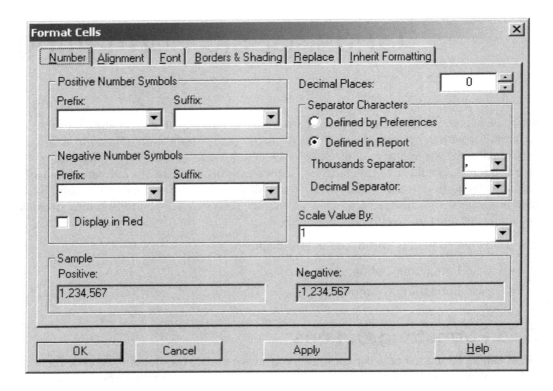

The number formatting options provide a variety of useful features, including the ability to set the following options:

- **Prefix** & **Suffixes** for positive and negative numbers – In many organizations, reports commonly utilize a standard set of numeric formatting options desired by company leadership. The ability to add a prefix and suffix to a positive or negative number provides the required flexibility needed to satisfy organizational requirements.

- **Display in Red** - In addition to the prefix and suffix settings, there is the ability to check the Display in Red checkbox. This displays negative numbers in red font. In some organizations, it is very common to see negative numbers displayed in parentheses and red formatting.

- **Scaling** - The **Scale Value By** option provides a solution to the very common scaling requirement imposed by many organizations. Corporate financial reports are commonly scaled in thousands or millions. The Scale Value By option provides the ability to modify the scaling of the numerical values in the report without having to impact the underlying application or perform a mathematical calculation in the report.

- **Defined by Preferences** – The Defined by Preferences option in the Separator Characters section is a unique option that allows for the formatting of displayed values to be defined by *unique users* in Workspace. These preferences can be changed by the user to display their preferred numeric display.

The sample section at the bottom of the window provides a preview for all of the changes made in the Number formatting tab.

Alignment & Indentation

The second formatting tab is for configuring **Alignment** settings, which see text and numeric values aligned in particular planes for selected cells in a grid.

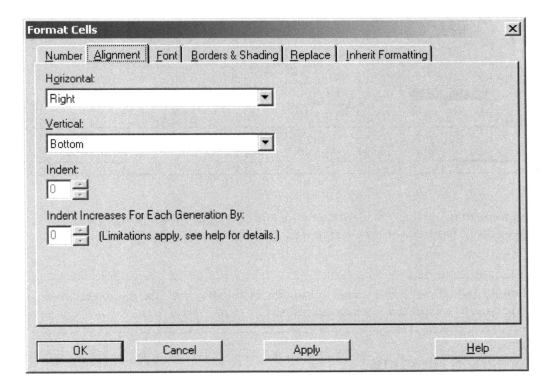

Alignment settings are used to set the horizontal and vertical display, as well as any indentation, for dimension values. Indentation settings control the indentation level for standard values as well as the increase in indentation for each hierarchical generation displayed in the report.

Fonts & Text Effects

The third formatting tab is the **Font** settings. It is used to format the text values for selected cells in a grid.

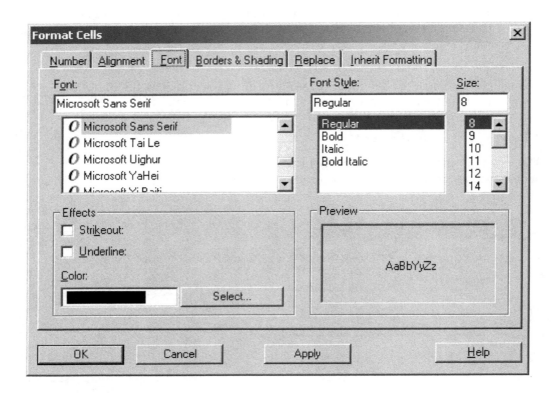

Font formatting provides standard font formatting controls. Notice how the ability to change color, basic text effects, and font characteristics only exists.

If the desired font size does not exist in the list of sizes, type the desired number into the box to set the font size manually.

Borders & Shading

The fourth tab - **Borders & Shading** - is used to configure the display of borders and shading.

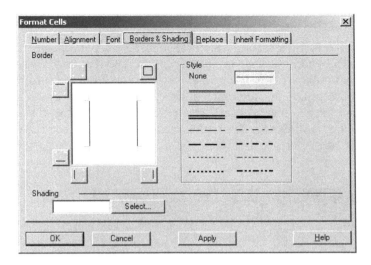

Borders and shading are commonly used in financial reports to segment content in the report, and are commonly seen when separating scenarios of data, totals, and variances.

Setting a border is completed by selecting a style of interest and clicking inside the border window to apply the style to the cell. The buttons outside the cell window are clicked to change cell formatting. Basic shading options can be configured by clicking the Select button next to the shading text box.

Cell Replacement

The fifth formatting tab is the **Replace** feature. It is used to replace values in a cell with a different value. This feature is commonly used to 'blank out' cells in a report, and is set by selecting the checkbox and either leaving the cell blank or typing in the value of interest.

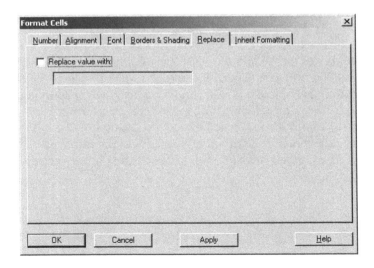

Inheriting Formatting

The final tab is **Inherit Formatting**. Inherit formatting is a complicated feature but provides significant benefits when formatting reports. The feature allows for the formatting of a particular section of a grid to be *inherited* (or copied) from another section in the grid. As such, this approach allows for the formatting of one section to serve as a template for all other sections, preventing the need to spend significant effort repeating formatting. It allows for formatting changes to take place in one area and cascade to the rest of the inherited objects.

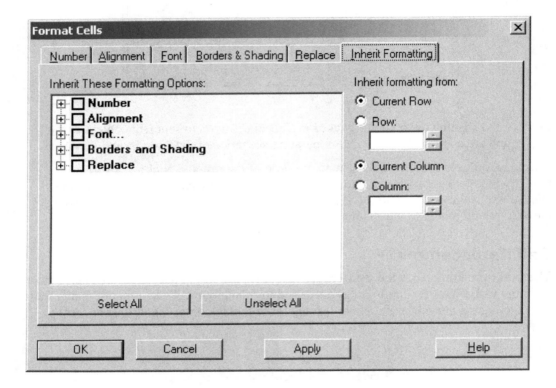

The different checkboxes on the left allow for the selection of a particular format to reuse. Inherit formatting from (on the right side of the screen) selects the area in the report from where formatting is copied, and it is commonly used when applying the same format across a set of rows or columns. In this case, desired formatting is applied to one row or column in the report manually and then all of the other rows with the same formatting needs can leverage its formatting. Changes to the initial row or column get propagated across all inherited rows or columns, providing improved report maintenance.

Example: Formatting a Grid

Formatting a grid with a quality display and setting up easy maintenance can be a chore for any report creator. The following example demonstrates a few techniques for formatting a grid quickly with a nice display and inherited formatting.

The first step in the process is to generate properly formatted headers for the grid. The following screenshot shows a grid without formatting.

Grid1				
◄	Years:Years	Time:Time	Transaction Type:Sale	Payment Type:User Point of View fc

		A	B	C	
		Original Price	Price Paid	Variance	
1	Personal Electronics	#	#	= #	
2	Home Entertainment	#	#	= #	
3	Other	#	#	= #	
4	Flat Panel	#	#	= #	
5	HDTV	#	#	= #	
6	Digital Recorders	#	#	= #	
7	Notebooks	#	#	= #	

After highlighting the header in Cell A, a bold format was applied using the Font formatting tab. A bottom border and grey shading were also applied using the Borders & Shading tab.

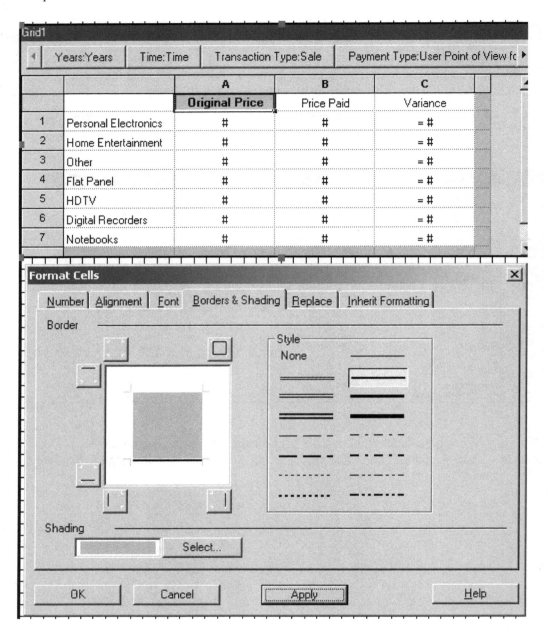

The next step in the formatting example is to separate the columns of data with left and right borders. This is completed by highlighting the entire Col A and setting the left and right border from the Borders & Shading formatting tab as shown in the following screenshot.

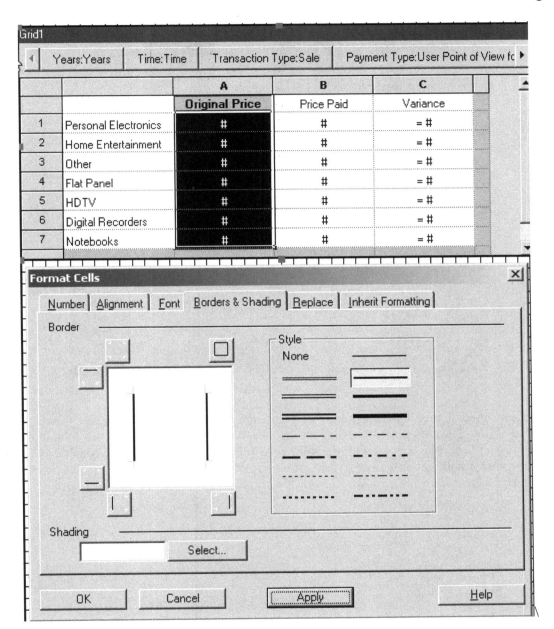

Continuing, the total line is formatted using a double line top border and a single line bottom border, which is completed by highlighting all of Row 8 and applying the chosen borders to the row as shown in the following screenshot.

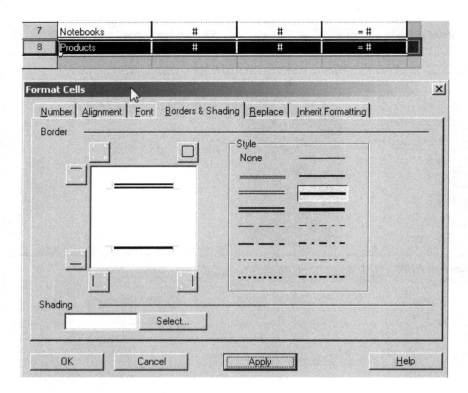

The last step is to highlight Col B and Col C and inherit the formatting from Col A and Current Row. The Current Row setting on the Inherit Formatting tab allows the column of each row to format in concert with the same row in Col A. The following screenshot shows the formatting configuration for Col B and Col C.

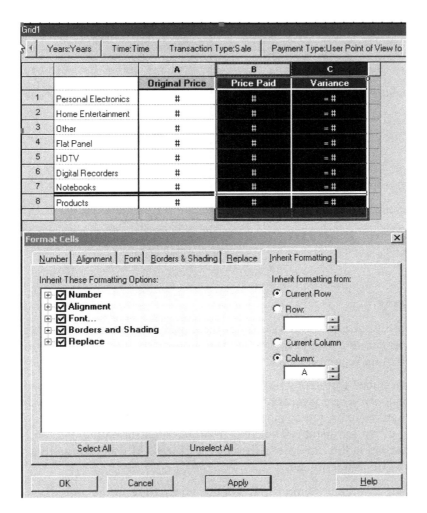

Once complete, running the report generates the following:

	Original Price	Price Paid	Variance
Personal Electronics	16,841,711	16,731,941	109,771
Home Entertainment	14,813,452	14,709,117	104,335
Other	4,166,050	4,138,863	27,188
Flat Panel	1,508,045	1,497,882	10,163
HDTV	5,390,138	5,350,020	40,117
Digital Recorders	818,360	812,788	5,572
Notebooks	1,634,730	1,623,587	11,144
Totals	35,821,213	35,579,920	241,293

Summary

While the concept of grid formatting is not the most exciting feature discussed in this book, an understanding of grid formatting techniques drives our ability to respond to the detailed formatting requirements of the user community.

Chapter 4 introduced formatting options and provided information about each tab of the formatting window. The concepts of number, alignment, font, borders and shading, and cell replacement were presented along with an example that demonstrated the approach to formatting a grid for display. The concept of inherited formatting was described and later demonstrated in the example to display the process of using formatting from one section of the grid as a template.

The formatting techniques demonstrated in this chapter are further demonstrated in Chapter 6: Conditional Formatting, and Chapter 9: Report Templates and Text Label Functions. Chapter 6 covers the same formatting options with conditional statements to provide more advanced reporting effects, and Chapter 9 digs into the concept of building a reporting template for standard reporting in an organization.

5

Grids: Advanced Member Selection & Formulas

Chapter 3, *Grids: Basic Operations, Charting, and the Point of View*, introduced the concept of configuring a grid and selecting members. While simple member selection options can be used to create well-designed reports, a set of advanced features exist for facilitating dynamic and complicated member selections. These advanced options provide the next step towards building a reporting template for use across the organization.

Additionally, Financial Reporting includes the ability to execute calculations and leverage functions, providing the functionality to create arithmetic operations and pull supplemental information from the system outside the simple grid configuration. Since this topic is vast, with a large set of features and combinations available for use, this chapter introduces a few common approaches and provides ideas for facilitating advanced features with the product.

The following content is introduced in this chapter:

- Advanced Member Selection
- Advanced Member Selection Examples
- Basic Formulas
- Formula Examples
- Text Rows, Columns, and Formulas
- Text Examples

Advanced Member Selection Settings

The applications that interface with Financial Reporting contain a dimensional structure, where each dimension is configured as a hierarchy. These hierarchies can be referenced using specific reporting logic to generate the desired view. Advanced member selection is the method used to select information dynamically from the hierarchy. Prompts and substitution variables are part of the advanced selection options and are also utilized to build dynamic reporting templates that respond well to requirements across the business.

Chapter 5

The example from the Chapter 3 is utilized to demonstrate the advanced member selection options. The following screenshot displays the example grid.

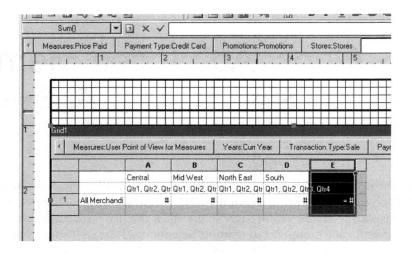

The example grid contains the All Merchandise member from the Products dimension in Row 1. While individual members from the dimension may be added to the report as separate rows, advanced member selection methods can be used to pick a defined set of information from a model using a function, variable, or prompt (effectively pulling the members into the report).

Within the example, double-clicking the All Merchandise member opens Select Members for the Products dimension, as per the following screenshot:

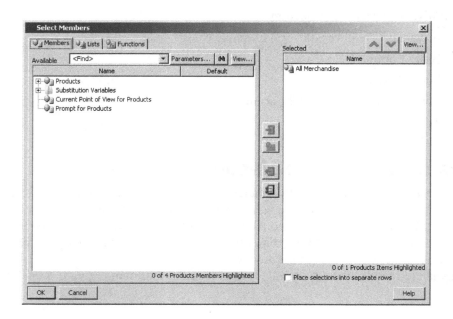

The Members tab provides a means to pull members directly from the hierarchy or through the use of substitution variables, prompts, lists, and functions.

Substitution Variables

One way to incorporate dynamic content into a report is through the use of **Substitution Variables** (if available). These variables are created in the source application and not in Financial Reporting, and the variables are typically created and managed by a system administrator. Using a variable stores a constant that is updatable in the application at any time. The variable approach is commonly used for dates, scenarios, and versions, and the approach is easily customizable to fit many reporting purposes. For example, instead of manually selecting the current month for the time dimension of a grid and then updating that report every month, a CurrMonth variable is created in the source data application and then updated each month. The variable can then be used in multiple reports to display the current month data and to support calculations and conditions. When it is time to update the month across all reports, the variable is changed in the application and all of the reports referencing the variable are subsequently updated. It is important to note that variables must be controlled by a user who has permission for the source application to update application variables, or who can use a process that loads the variables into the application through scripting.

Current Point of View

The next item in the member selection window is the **Current Point of View**. This adds the dimension into the Point of View and allows the current Point of View's value for the dimension to be used in the report. For example, when the Current Point of View for Products (in the example grid) is selected for the Products dimension, the Products dimension is added to the Point of View. Accordingly, a user running a report may control the content displayed directly in the grid during runtime and reports are less reliant on hardcoding. This approach also facilitates a reduction in maintenance since grid selection is now dynamic, and an organization can use this feature in a template without needing to create multiple versions of the same report. An example of the Current Point of View is demonstrated at the end of this section.

Prompts

The third option is to **Prompt** the user for selection during runtime. This approach is very similar to using a Current Point of View for the grid, but the prompt feature may be applied to allow multiple selections for one dimension. This approach allows some customization and flexibility that the Current Point of View does not provide, but the prompt feature may become confusing to users not familiar with the report. Training users for a prompt-based report takes additional time due to the complexity of selecting values for prompts.

Prompt-based approaches are commonly tied with formulas, allowing the user to select a member from the prompt so that another column can derive a subsequent value. For example, creating a prompt for month and then creating a formula in the second column to grab the value of the prior month is a commonly used approach. An example of prompts is also demonstrated at the end of this section.

Lists & Functions

The List tab is the second tab in the Select Members window. A list accesses a set of values from the dimension based on the dimension layout. One of the most commonly used lists is the *Level 0* list, which provides the complete set of bottom level members from the dimension. Notice in the screenshot, below, any level or generation can be selected from the Lists tab. Lists are helpful when attempting to grab a set of members from a ragged hierarchy (which is commonly seen in many Hyperion applications).

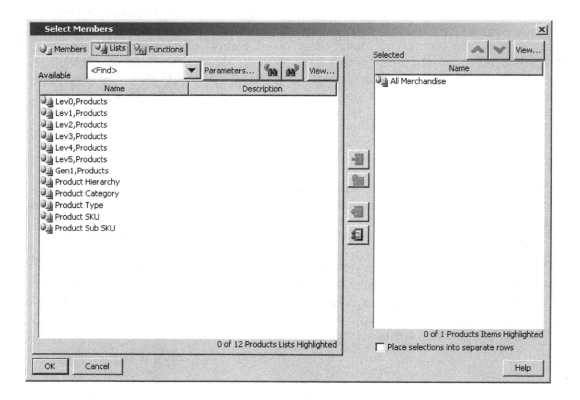

The final set of options for selecting members is through the **Functions** tab. Functions provide a range of different options for deriving a set of members. The following screenshot shows the Select Members window open on the Functions tab.

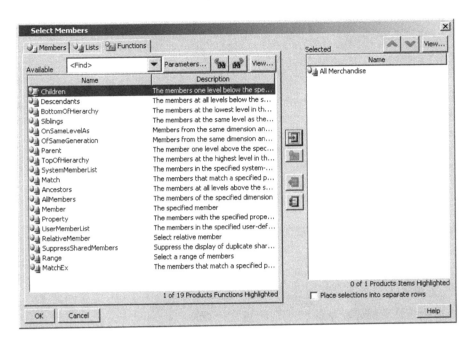

Functions contain syntax that is commonly seen with most multidimensional systems. Notice the ability to derive Children, Descendants, or the Parent of a member in the hierarchy. Functions are utilized by selecting the desired function from the left pane of the window and pressing the arrow button (left-to-right) to bring the function into the selected pane. Upon pressing the button, an edit window opens which is specific to the function selected, as shown in the following screenshot.

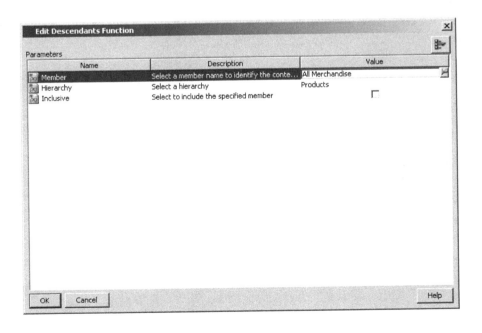

The edit function window is different for each function and provides the arguments and options available for the function. In the example above, the options for the Descendants function are displayed. The function takes in three arguments: Member, Hierarchy, and Inclusive.

The edit window for this function provides a selection box, allowing for the selection of values from the application instead of typing directly into the window. In the following example, the member All Merchandise is selected. Once the OK button is pushed, the edit window updates the syntax of the Select Members window with the chosen configuration. The following screenshot shows the display once Descendants of the member All Merchandise is selected.

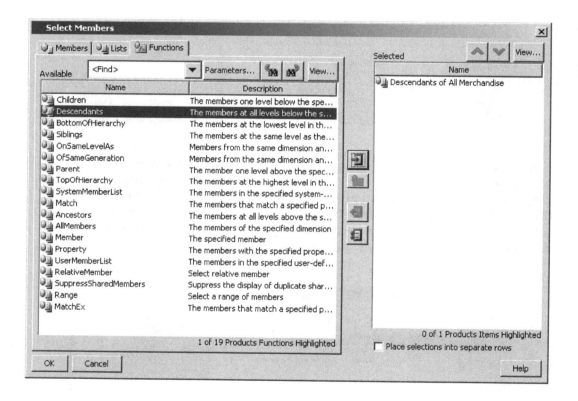

Combining Functions, Lists, and Members

Selections from the Functions, Lists, and Members tab of the hierarchy may be utilized together with operators, parentheses, and inverse (i.e. *not*) logic. The following example demonstrates an example grid that pulls all Level 0 Products *not* from the entire hierarchy but from a *section* of the hierarchy.

This capability is demonstrated through the use of the same example, where only the level 0 members of the All Merchandise section of the hierarchy are chosen. With the

Descendants of All Merchandise selected, the next step is to open the Lists tab and add the Lev0, Products list item into the selected area as shown here.

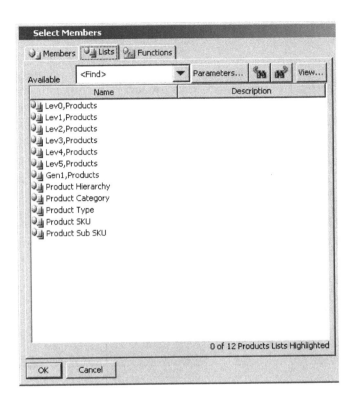

The selected area now shows the list and the function, with the And operator signifying that members are returned when both conditions are satisfied.

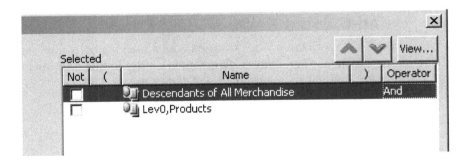

> Inverse, parenthesis, and operator features are displayed by right-clicking in the selected window or by pressing the View button (see the screenshot above) and selecting Advanced.

When the report is run, the grid shows only the level 0 members of the All Merchandise section of the hierarchy. Conversely, to not show level 0 members in the report, selecting the Not checkbox next to the Lev0,Products section would display all upper-level members in the All Merchandise hierarchy.

Wildcards in Functions

Another advanced feature is the concept of using a wildcard (*) with functions that allow text inputs. In Hyperion applications, different prefixes are commonly used in dimensions. When using the Match function (typically used to find members in a hierarchy) the wildcard is used to pull only specific dimension members that start, end, or contain a set of characters. The following screenshot shows an example that pulls descendants from the Products dimension for members that only start with an M.

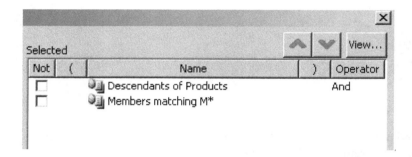

Example: Using Current Point of View

The Current Point of View is effective when coupled with a member selection function to create a dynamic way to choose and display members in a grid. In this example, the first row from the grid in the following screenshot is updated to use the Descendants member function and the Current Point of View for the Products dimension.

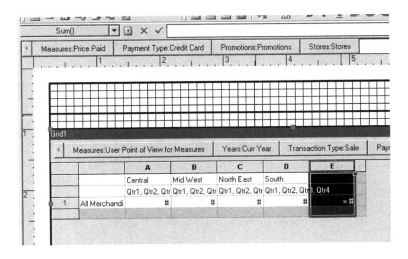

Double-clicking on the All Merchandise value in Row 1 opens the member selection window for the row. Instead of selecting a value from the members tab, the functions tab is opened and the Descendants value is selected.

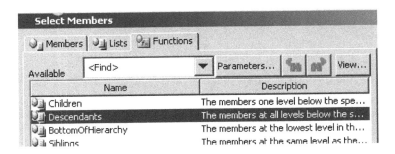

After bringing the Descendants function into the selected area, the Edit Descendants Function window appears. Instead of setting the member to a fixed value, the Current Point of View option for the dimension is selected to allow the user to pick the list of descendants to display during runtime. When clicking the Value section for Member, an icon appears that opens the member selection window and allows the member selection for the dimension. Selecting Current Point of View for Products populates the window as shown below.

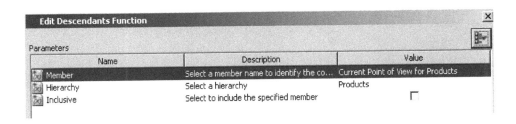

Once complete, the grid displays the text of the function in the grid, as shown in the following screenshot.

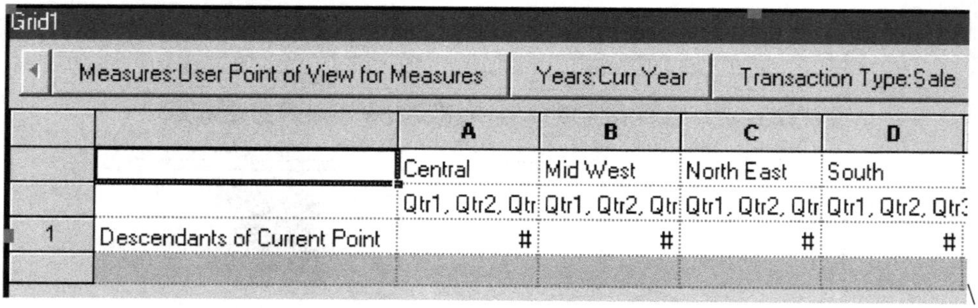

At runtime, the User Point of View allows the user to select a value for the Products dimension. The following screenshot shows the Point of View with the Products selection box updated to show Personal Electronics.

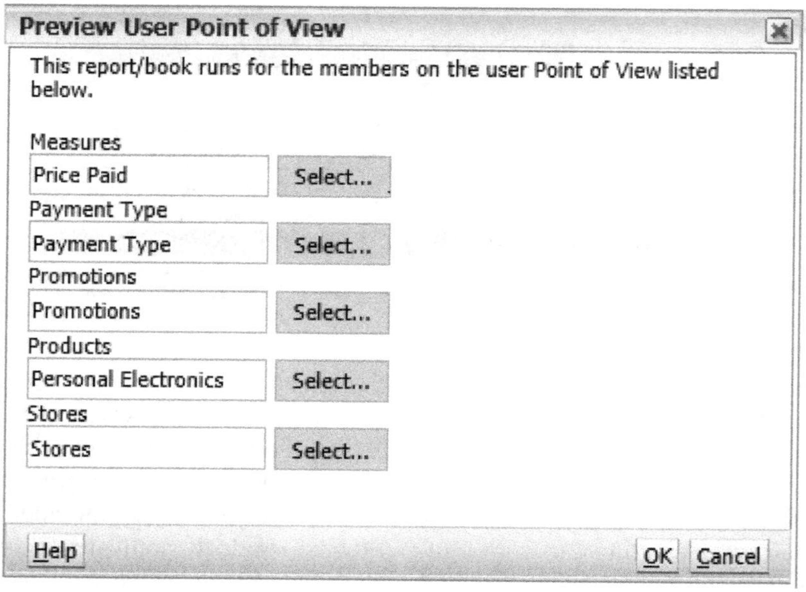

The descendants of the Personal Electronics member now appear in the report.

HomePage	Chapter 5 - Current Point of View ✕		

/Chap5/Chapter 5 - Current Point of View

Measures: Price Paid	Payment Type: Payment Type	Promotions: Promotions	Produc

Years: Curr Year Transaction Typ

	North East				
	Qtr1	Qtr2	Qtr3	Qtr4	
Digital Cameras	319,032	309,814	97,049	0	
Camcorders	693,122	629,911	176,030	0	
Photo Printers	304,038	300,392	91,185	0	
Digital Cameras/Camcorders	1,316,191	1,240,117	364,264	0	
Handhelds	0	0	0	0	
Memory	602,217	596,285	179,934	0	
Other Accessories	1,483,535	1,501,946	452,318	0	
Handhelds/PDAs	2,085,752	2,098,231	632,252	0	
Boomboxes	399,657	395,440	118,150	0	
Radios	377,118	376,569	117,023	0	

Example: Using Prompts

Prompts are a great feature that supports the requirement for selectable, dynamic, and varying dimension members in a grid. This example shows how to configure the prior example with a selectable prompt for the measure displayed in each row of the report. Using the same example report used for the Current Point of View, another data row was inserted to allow for the configuration of two prompts.

Grid1

		Measures:User Point of View for Measures	Years:Curr Year	Tra
			A	B	C
			Central	Mid West	North Ea
			Qtr1, Qtr2, Qtr	Qtr1, Qtr2, Qtr	Qtr1, Qtr
	1	Descendants of Current Point	#	#	
	2	Descendants of Current Point	#	#	

Currently, the Measures dimension is set for selection from the Point of View and a user can only select one member with the current setup. This example modifies the grid to move the Measures dimension into rows using the dimension layout for the grid.

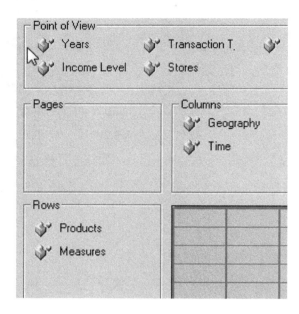

For ease of demonstration, the descendants function was removed from the Products dimension in both rows to only show the Current Point of View for Products as the selected member. This change was made to more easily display the output during runtime.

The following screenshot displays the grid correctly configured for the rows.

Prompts are applied by selecting the Measures member in each row individually and selecting the Prompt option from the selection window. Double-clicking the Measures cell for Row 1 opens the Member selection window as shown.

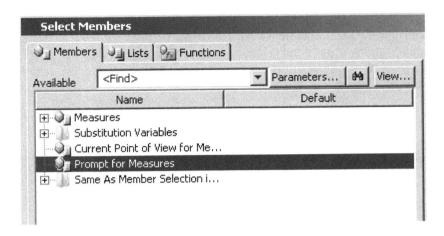

Selecting Prompt for Measures, moves it into the selected area, and pressing the OK button opens a new window to define the prompts. The following window displays the prompt configured for the Measures prompt on Row 1.

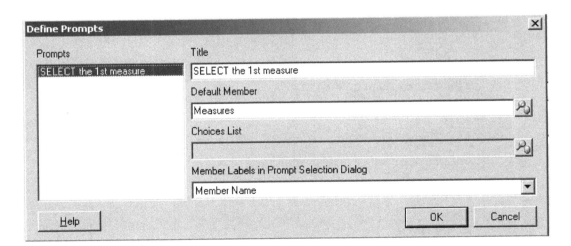

The Define Prompts window allows for customization with the following options:

- Title – Used for the display on the prompt selection window at runtime. It is useful to provide a good text description as shown in the example.

- Default Member – The Default Member is applied when the prompt is displayed to the user at runtime.

- Choices List – Restricts the user to a defined set of members at runtime. It is configured by pressing the magnifying glass button.
- Member Labels in Prompt Selection Dialog – Allows the user to select from the Member Name, Alias, or both.

Once the configuration is complete for the first row, the FR studio grid updates and shows Prompt for Measures in the grid. The steps above were followed again to add the second prompt, with a different title and description. Once complete, the grid updates as shown below.

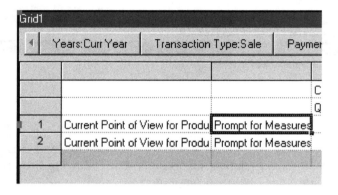

When the report is run, the first display is the User Point of View for the report, as shown:

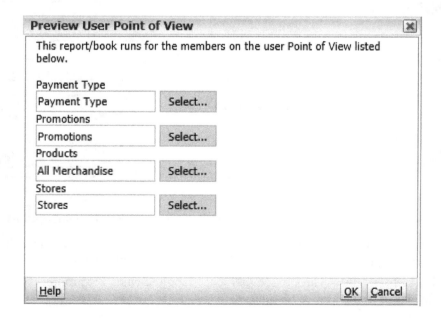

After the selection of the User Point of View is complete, the Respond to Prompts window appears for the selection of each prompt. Notice each prompt is listed individually with the titles configured in the earlier steps. In this example, the default members are switched to Original Price for the prompt in Row 1 and Price Paid for the prompt in Row 2.

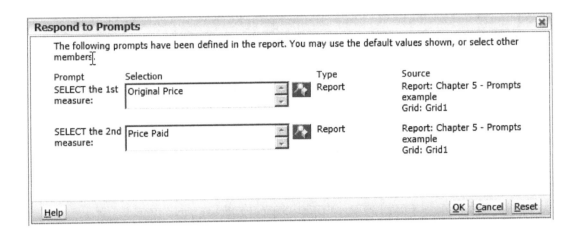

When the report runs, the grid displays with the dynamic selections listed in the first two rows.

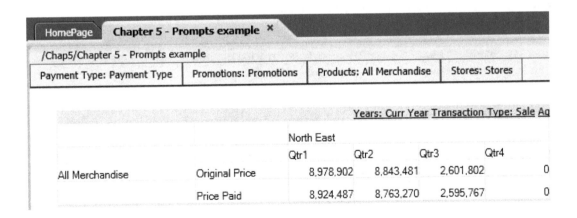

Basic Formulas

Formulas provide a means to modify content displayed in a report. There are a number of formulas built into Financial Reporting, and they offer a means of performing a variety of advanced calculations. This section demonstrates the use of basic formula calculations in a grid.

The following screenshot shows the example grid from the previous chapter, where four columns exist with one geographical value for each column. Adding a new formula column is similar to adding a new column of data, and is completed by selecting a column, right-clicking and selecting Insert Column → Formula as shown in the following screenshot.

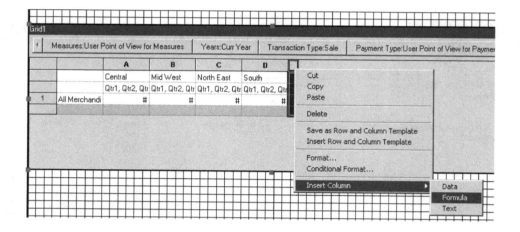

Notice the new column is added to the report with the two header rows displaying blank cells while the cell in *Row 1* is shown with the following notation =#. The =# notation denotes that the value in the intersection is a formula. The **Formula** bar is also now editable as highlighted in the following screenshot.

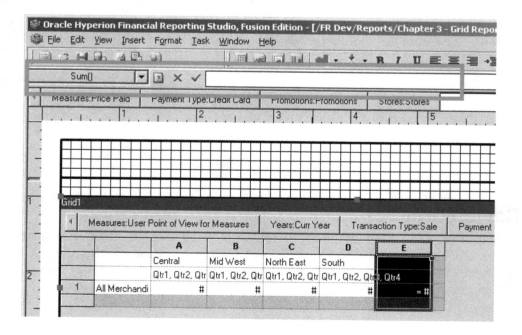

A function is added by directly typing into the formula bar or by selecting a function at the beginning of the formula bar. Using a simple example, the configuration of a Sum function is completed by selecting Sum and using the notation of the appropriate column values. In this example, Col A through Col D are built into the Sum function with the function text denoted as Sum([A:D]) as shown in the following screenshot.

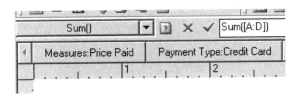

After entering a function into the function bar, the green checkbox to the left of the function textbox must be pressed when complete. If the green checkbox is not pressed, the changes to the formula are lost.

A number of variations for adding columns can be used to generate a similar outcome. These include simple arithmetic [A]+[B] or the use of row identifiers Sum([1]). Once the formula is complete, running the report displays as follows.

ale Age: Age Income Level: Income Level										
North East				South					Sum([A:D])	
Qtr1	Qtr2	Qtr3	Qtr4	Qtr1	Qtr2	Qtr3	Qtr4			
0	3,558,216	3,470,356	1,080,226	0	2,652,971	2,674,500	791,794	0	14,228,063	

Export In Query-Ready Mode

The Financial Reporting documentation provides information on all of the functions available for use in the product. This chapter provides a few examples at the end of this section to demonstrate a set of common and useful functions.

Custom Headings

In the example in the screenshot above, the syntax of the Sum function is displayed in the report layout as a heading. While this feature is useful for troubleshooting and editing the report, the addition of a **Custom Heading** provides a way to display a custom text label instead of function syntax.

Selecting the heading cell for the function brings up the Column Properties window, and selecting the Custom Heading radio button and populating the text All Geographies overwrites the function syntax with the new label. If no text is desired, the custom heading can be left blank, removing the label from the column altogether.

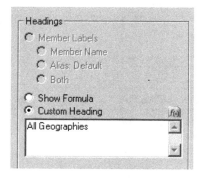

Custom headings can be applied to any heading member in a grid; not just formula columns.

Overriding Formulas

The formula in the previous example was applied to the entire column. In certain situations, the formula may need to be varied across the rows. Selecting the cell of interest brings up the *Cell Properties* window for a cell containing a function, as shown in the following screenshot.

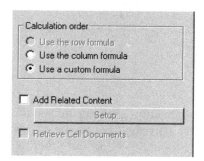

The ability to Use the Column Formula or Use a Custom Formula exists for the cell. Selecting Use a Custom Formula enables the Formula bar for the individual cell to be modified while the remaining cells use the column formula.

Formula Errors

Creating functions with complexity may result in syntax errors when building calculations. The following screenshot shows a sample calculation with an error message.

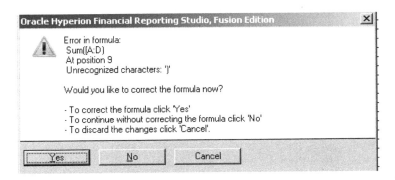

Financial Reporting offers a degree of intelligence when evaluating and alerting the user to errors in a formula. In the example above, a right bracket is missing from the Sum formula, and the Financial Reporting editor tells us that an unrecognized character has appeared and the position of the unrecognized character. Be sure to select the desired button of interest (Yes, No, or Cancel) button when editing the errant formula.

Using Row and Column References

Formula rows and columns can refer to other columns, rows, and even specific cells from other grids in a single grid. Below are some examples of the syntax used to reference a row column and specific cells.

- Col[A]
- [A,1]
- [A]
- Row[1]
- [1]
- Current
- Grid1.[A,1]
- Grid1.[1]

Unless a specific cell is desired, avoid using the specific cell reference, e.g. [A,1] and instead use the column reference [A] or row reference [1]. Also notice the values that use the grid name in front of the reference, e.g. Grid1.[A,1]. This syntax is used to pull a value from one grid into another grid, requiring the reference of the grid name in the syntax. Chapter 8, *Advanced Techniques* demonstrates the use of these concepts in more detail.

Example: If/Then Conditional Function

The **If/Then** function is very powerful and allows a formula row or column to perform an activity following the evaluation of a condition. A desired activity occurs specific to passing or failing the condition. The syntax for this function is:

```
IfThen(condition, value if condition is true, value if false)
```

The If/Then formula may be used to perform a variety of operations including arithmetic expressions. When using the If/Then function to perform arithmetic operations, the **Eval** function must also be included for the function to execute the mathematical expression.

In the following example, a formula is created in Col D to calculate the variance percentage between Col A and Col B for each row displayed, as long as Col B is not equal to 0. If Col B is equal to 0 then the arithmetic operation fails since the formula cannot divide by zero. In this example, the If/Then formula is used to evaluate if Col B is 0 to prevent the errant arithmetic formula and replace the output with a 0 when experienced.

The Variance Percent column is created by adding a new formula column to the grid with the custom header Variance Percent. With the entire column selected, the following formula is entered and the cells formatted to show decimal values and the % sign:

```
IfThen([B]=0,0,Eval(([A]-[B])/[B]*100))
```

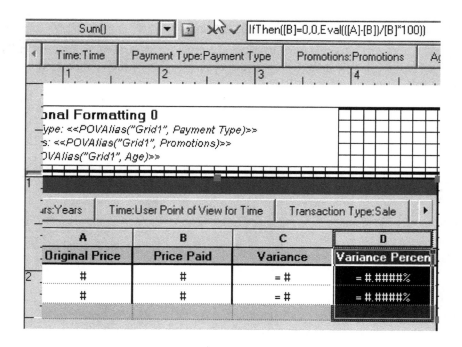

Using the sample syntax, the following deconstructs the function.

```
IfThen([B]=0 (condition), 0 (value if true), Eval(([A]-[B])/[B]*100))
(value if false))
```

Notice the first argument in the function tests to see if B=0. If the condition evaluates to *true*, any row displaying 0 in the output of the report displays the second argument, which is the number 0. If the condition in argument 1 displays as *false*, the mathematical evaluation Eval(([A]-[B])/[B]*100)) is displayed.

Additionally, the ability exists to test more than one condition in the argument. These conditions can also be nested with parentheses. As a simple example, the following function shows the same example but the logical condition is updated to a range.

```
IfThen(([B]<1 AND [B]>0),0,Eval(([A]-[B])/[B]*100))
```

Notice the extra set of parentheses and the use of the AND operator. Additionally the OR operator and the not operator (<> or !) may be used in the expressions to create more complex arguments.

Text Formulas, Rows, and Columns

A column or row of text can be added to a grid to display a simple text label or a formula that derives a text value. Adding a **Text** column to a grid is similar to adding a data or formula column and completed by highlighting a column on the grid, right-clicking, and selecting Insert Column → Text as shown here.

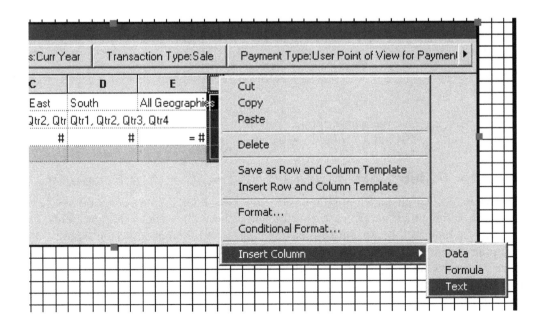

Using a simple example, highlighting the cell of interest for the text column opens the cell properties window with the ability to add text-related content. Simply typing into the box displays text on the report as shown in the following screenshot.

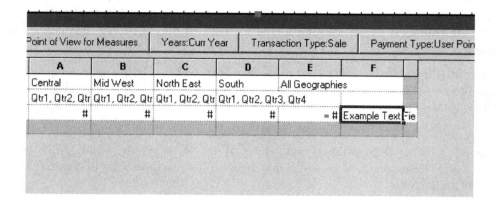

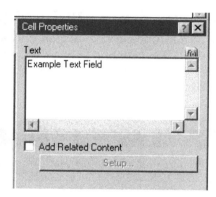

These text cells can also include formulas. The following sections of this chapter provide examples of pulling text values from an application using formulas.

Example: Pulling Attributes using the Member Property

In Hyperion applications, attribute dimensions may exist that display descriptive information about a member. In reports referencing these dimensions, requirements commonly include adding attribute dimension values for members onto the report. Adding the attribute dimension to the grid directly through the dimension layout can start to have a negative impact on performance as well as cause the report to become overly complex. To remedy this, a text function is used to pull the member property associated with an attribute dimension member.

The function used to pull an Attribute member onto a report is the **MemberProperty** function, which takes the following arguments:

```
<<MemberProperty("Grid_Name", Row/Col/Page, Dimension_Name, Property)>>
```

The syntax for the function is relatively straightforward with the exception of `Property`, which refers to the name of the attribute dimension in this case. Referring to the sample application used throughout the book and the attribute dimensions that exist, the following demonstrates the appropriate values for a text cell:

```
<<MemberProperty("grid1", 1, Products, Area Code)>>
```

Note that the dimension specified needs to line up with the data cell referenced in the second argument, which in this example is the Products dimension. At runtime, if an area code exists, as per the attribute dimension, then the appropriate area code value is pulled by the function and displayed in the report. Below is a screenshot showing the function and its inclusion into a text column cell.

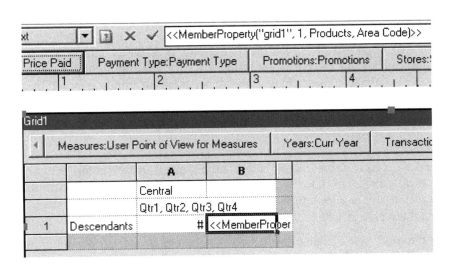

When the report is run, each row displays the Product and its corresponding Area Code attribute value.

Example: Pulling Cell Text from Hyperion Planning

Hyperion Planning applications contain text-based values that provide supporting information for the preparation of budgets, forecasts, and other planning scenarios. This example demonstrates the functionality used to pull Cell Text. **Cell Text** resides at a distinct intersection of the Hyperion Planning application.

When displaying Cell Text, the database connection for the grid must be a Hyperion Planning application and not the underlying Essbase application since the Cell Text is stored in the Hyperion Planning relational database tables and *not* the Essbase application directly.

Adding cell text to a report is completed by adding a text row or column to a grid connected to a Hyperion Planning database. The default Cell Text function displays as follows:

```
<<CellText("GridName", Row, Col, Page)>>
```

An example of configuring the cell text function for the current intersection of Row 1, Col A is displayed as follows, where the selections in the point of view complete the intersection.

```
<<CellText("Grid1", 1, A, 1)>>
```

Additionally, the concept of the **current** value may be used for the rows to make a function more dynamic. This current value allows the cell text to use the row value of the current row. The same function can be used in one column instead of having to create a separate evaluation for each data row added to the grid in FR Studio.

```
<<CellText("Grid1", current, A, 1)>>
```

The Cell Text function is a strong feature, commonly used when reporting on Hyperion Planning applications that have users entering cell text. Leveraging this function with designed reports enhances the display with the pertinent information stored in the application.

Summary

As Financial Reporting gains traction across an organization, the complexity of reporting requests typically increase. The use of advanced member selection and formulas provides a way to better support the more complicated requests of the business, while reducing maintenance efforts.

The chapter started with explanations of advanced member selection techniques using Substitution Variables, the Current Point of View, and Prompts. The chapter reviewed Functions and Lists in member selection with an example that integrated both with advanced selection criteria. Two examples were offered at the end of the section to demonstrate the use of the Current Point of View and Prompts using practical examples.

The chapter continued with an overview of using formulas in grids, with detail into cell references, approaches to configuration, and formula features. The chapter demonstrated an example of using the IF/Then formula with conditional operators to show the power of formulas in reports. The chapter then moved on to the concept of using a text column for the display of text or dynamic content through the use of text-based formulas.

We wrapped things up with two powerful text formula examples, including the referencing of attributes and Hyperion Planning cell text. While the content and examples in this chapter just scratched the surface on the functionality that can be demonstrated with the product, the information (along with the product documentation) should position report builders with the necessary knowledge to leverage the full suite of formulas and functions.

6

Conditional Formatting

Conditional formatting is broadly defined as the concept of highlighting cells based on a set of conditions to draw attention to a particular set of data. Financial Reporting takes conditional formatting a step further and provides significantly greater control when formatting any value returned in a grid. The software provides common spotlighting features, but it also allows for the modification of alignment, number and text formats, borders and shading, and cell replacement.

The use of advanced conditional logic with formatting is available, providing the ability to use cell values, dimensional positions, and many other features as conditions. This conditional formatting feature allows for a wide range of formatting options and the ability to reduce development time by utilizing the feature along with dynamic cell functions. This chapter demonstrates the concepts of conditional formatting and provides examples to demonstrate the use of common conditional formatting operations.

The following content is introduced in this chapter:

- Conditional Format Interface
- Formats and Conditions
- Dimension Formatting
- Spotlighting
- Member Replacement

Conditional Format Interface

Conditional formatting can be added to rows, columns, and even individual cells in a financial report. Conditional formatting is added by selecting the grid area of interest and selecting **Conditional Format** from the Format menu or by right-clicking and selecting Conditional Format from the right-click menu as shown in the following screenshot.

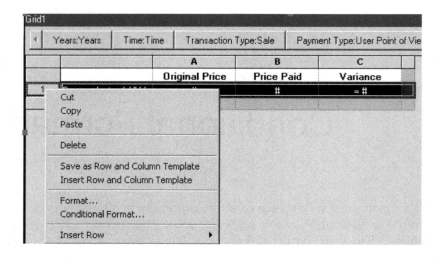

Upon selecting the Conditional Format menu item, the Conditional Format window appears as shown in the following screenshot.

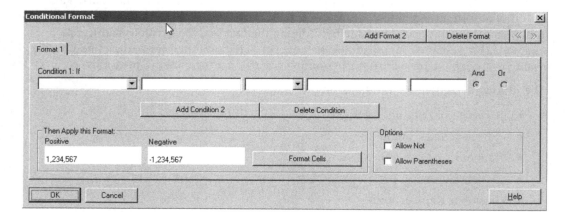

Formats

The Conditional Format window appears simple in design, but significant flexibility is contained inside the interface. The interface begins with a single format tab (entitled Format 1). Each desired format for selected cells is split into separate format tabs, allowing the user to set *different formats* across the same area. Notice each tab controls a different formatting display and *not* the set of rules for the condition. The set of rules for the condition is specified inside each tab (specific for each format).

The format for each tab is configured by selecting the Format Cells button at the bottom of the window, which opens the Format Cells window shown in the following screenshot.

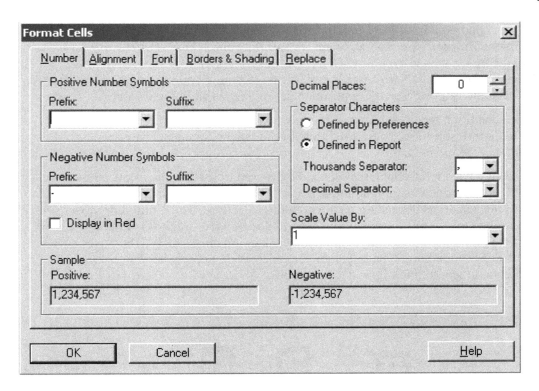

The Format Cells window is similar to the formatting window discussed earlier in the book, except that the *Inherit Formating* tab is not included. Conditional formatting can be used to customize the Number format as well as Alignment, Font, Borders & Shading, and value replacements. Upon selecting the format tab of interest and pressing the OK button to close the window, the main conditional formatting window opens to display the selected positive and negative number formatting.

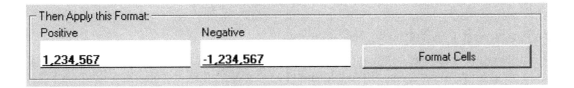

Conditions

Formats are based on conditions, which are used to segment and define the set of values to format. Conditions are set by using the condition boxes in the middle of the interface. Notice the word If next to the Condition 1 text label. The text signifies that the format is applied *If and only If* the applied conditions are met.

The first condition drop-down box [marked as 1, below] is for setting the type of condition. The most common types are for specific values, but Member Names, Alias, Generation, Level, and even Auto Calculation can be formatted. These options are differentiators within the software's conditional formatting options, over other software, as formatting can be based off application definitions, in addition to values.

Once a condition type is selected, four input boxes (to the right of the condition) are configured for selection. These condition drop-down boxes update based on the condition type selected.

Continuing from left to right, the second box is used to set the dimension, application selection, or formula to apply to the condition. The third box is for the operator, which is text or mathematical depending on the previous selections. The fourth drop-down is used to describe the value of the condition (used to describe the fifth box) or the value itself. The fifth box is used to set the value that the condition must satisfy. The boxes become disabled if the condition type or parameters selected do not require their use. The following screenshot highlights each input box.

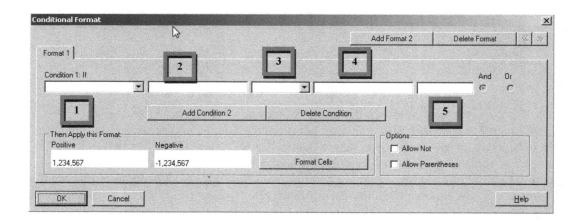

Advanced Condition Features

Multiple conditions with logic and operators may be added to the Format tab to control a wide range of requirements. These additional conditions allow for building in the **AND**, **OR**, and **NOT** conditions as well as parentheses. Additional conditions are added and deleted by using the Add Condition and Delete Condition buttons.

Upon adding a new condition, a new row is added below the previous condition and the AND/OR operator sections of the previous condition become active. Pressing the Delete Condition button prompts a menu to select the condition to remove. The following screenshot shows the Conditional Format window with two conditions prepared.

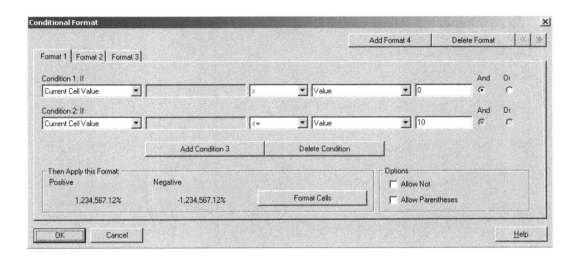

The condition above is a very common conditional formatting example. It tests a cell value to determine if the value returned is within a particular range. In this case an AND operator is used to test if the Current Cell Value is greater than 0 AND less than or equal to 10. In addition to using the AND or OR operators, the NOT operator and Parentheses can be added to the interface by selecting the Allow Not and Allow Parentheses checkboxes at the bottom of the window.

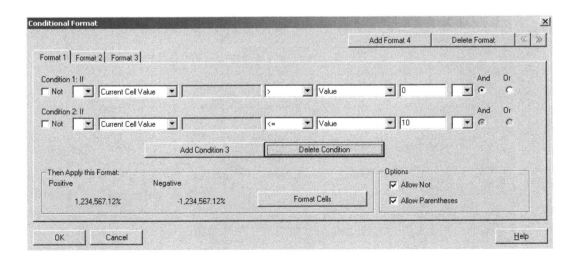

Chapter 6

Notice the new Not checkbox at the beginning of each condition statement and the two empty drop-downs at the beginning and end of each condition. The Not checkbox is used to execute the inverse of a statement. For instance, in Condition #3 (below) formatting is inactive when the Current Cell Value equals 5.

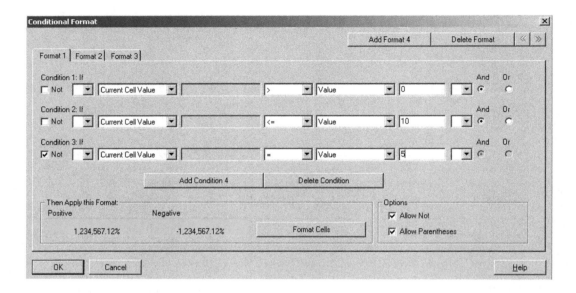

In our next example, parentheses and the OR statement are used to separate the first two conditions from the second two conditions.

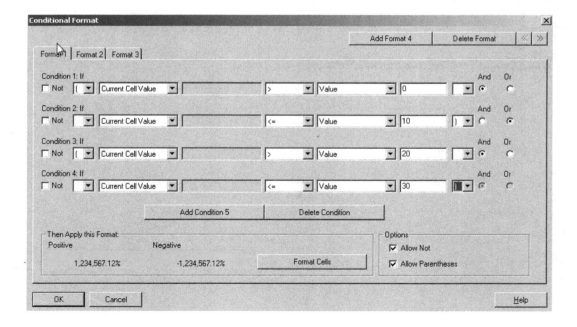

In this example, the Format tab is true if Conditions 1 and 2 are satisfied, or Conditions 3 and 4 are satisfied. Notice the use of the two single parentheses at the beginning of Condition 1, the end of Condition 2; the beginning of Condition 3, and the end of Condition 4. More complicated uses of parentheses can also be configured. The following screenshot is a more complicated example to highlight the use of nested parentheses.

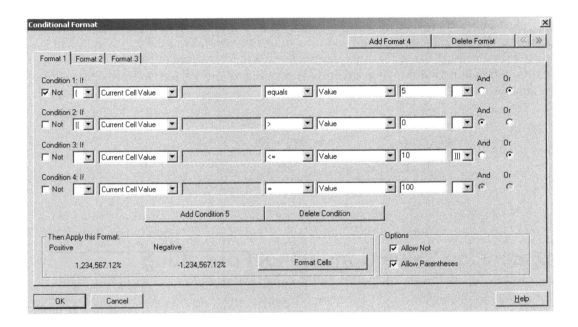

Nesting conditions are easily completed by using multiple parentheses. Parentheses can be four levels deep. Since adding parentheses may result in complicated logic, Financial Reporting prompts the user with error messages in the event of a parenthesis mismatch.

Order of Precedence

Each cell may contain only *one* conditional formatting configuration. Attempts to overlay a row or column with an additional set of conditional formatting generates a user prompt to remove the existing conditional formatting before applying the new formatting.

There are situations where the conditions in each format tab may overlap with conditions in other format tabs. When conditions overlap, an order of precedence is evaluated with Format 1 being the first condition evaluated, then Format 2, and so on through the list of formats. The Conditional Format window contains two buttons in the upper right-hand corner for changing the order of the format tabs. While on a format tab, the >> and << arrows (shown in the following screenshot) are used to move a format from one position to another in the format tab order.

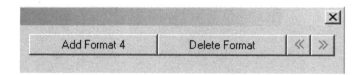

Dimension Value Conditional Formatting

One of the unique benefits to conditional formatting is the ability to apply specific formatting to dimension values based on the generation or level of the values returned in the report. In the following example, a grid is created with the Descendants of All Merchandise (Products Dimension), and Original Price, Price Paid, and Variance columns as shown:

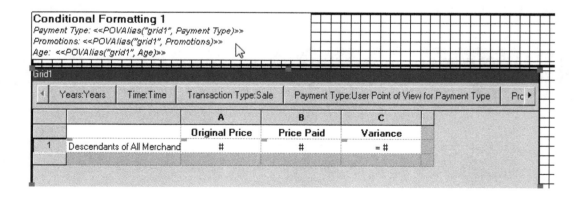

In this example, conditional formatting was applied to the entire first row. Each formatting condition was applied to the entire row and contains one condition, configured to use the Generation value of the member. Since the first row of the grid contains the descendants function, multiple rows are returned during runtime. The use of the generation condition provides the ability to format members differently based on their position in the dimensional hierarchy. The following condition shows Format 1, configured using the generation condition.

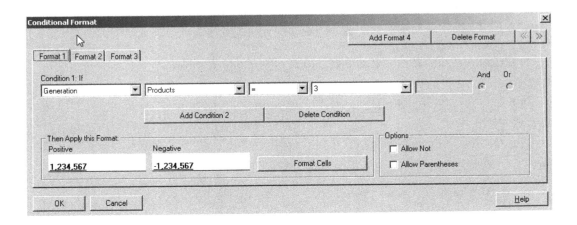

When the grid is displayed at runtime, the conditional formatting utility inspects each row and applies a bold font type, underline, and bottom border to each row where the generation of the member returned from the descendants function is at the third level from the top of the Products dimension. All rows (where the generation of the Products member is not equal to 3) receive standard grid formatting.

Format 2 uses the same generation function approach but applies specific formatting to generation 4.

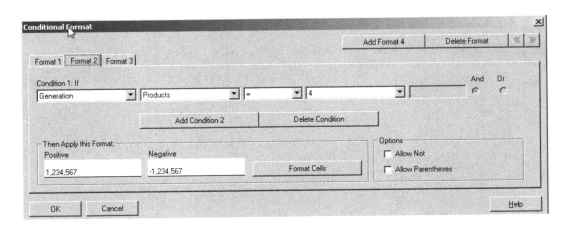

In Format 2, the numbers are left in default formatting except for application of a bottom border. Additionally, an indentation is set to indent the values returned from the generation to better represent the hierarchy as shown in the following screenshot.

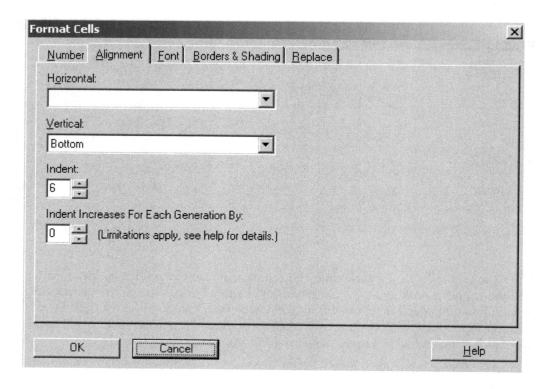

Format 3 continues with the same logic where the condition references generation 5.

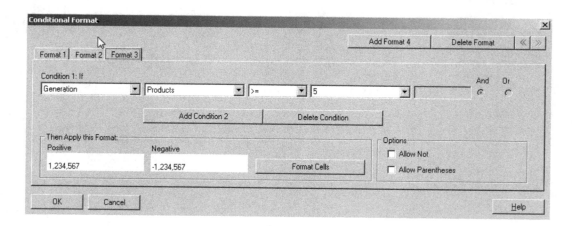

When the condition in Format 3 is met, only indentation is applied.

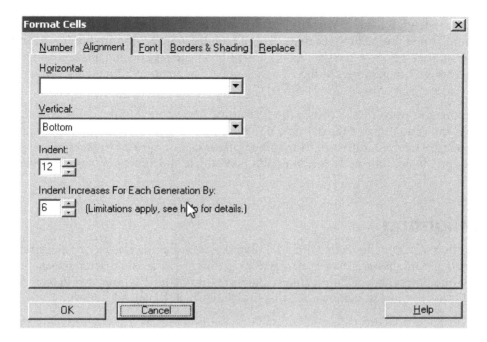

Running the report displays the following formatting.

Conditional Formatting 1
Payment Type: Payment Type
Promotions: Newspaper Ad
Age: Age

<ins>Years: Years</ins> <ins>Time: Time</ins> <ins>Transaction Type: Sale</ins> <ins>Income Level: Income Level</ins> <ins>Stores:</ins>
<ins>Stores</ins> <ins>Geography: Geography</ins>

		Original Price	Price Paid	Variance
	Digital Cameras	16,196	14,576	1,620
	Camcorders	30,264	27,238	3,026
	Photo Printers	17,316	15,584	1,732
Digital Cameras/Camcorders		63,776	57,398	6,378
	Handhelds	0	0	0
	Memory	36,679	33,011	3,668
	Other Accessories	87,881	79,092	8,788
Handhelds/PDAs		124,560	112,104	12,456
	Boomboxes	20,330	18,297	2,033
	Radios	23,147	20,833	2,314
Portable Audio		43,477	39,130	4,347
Personal Electronics		**231,812**	**208,632**	**23,181**

Notice the indentation and formatting differences for each row. Personal Electronics is a Generation 3 member, which receives the bold, underline, and bottom border. Members at the Portable Audio row are generation 4 members, and receive indentation and a bottom border. The members at the Radios level are generation 5 members, which receive indentation only.

It is imporant to point out that since the formatting was applied to the entire row in this example, the formatting of the numeric columns are also indented. If indenting numeric columns is not desired, different formatting options can be applied to the dimension column and the numeric columns, to apply indenting to the dimension values column alone.

Spotlighting

Spotlighting is displaying cells with a highlighted color based on a set of values returned in a report. Spotlighting is commonly used to highlight variances, discrepancies, or positive outcomes through color. In this example, simple red, yellow, and green spotlights are applied to demonstrate this functionality in Financial Reporting.

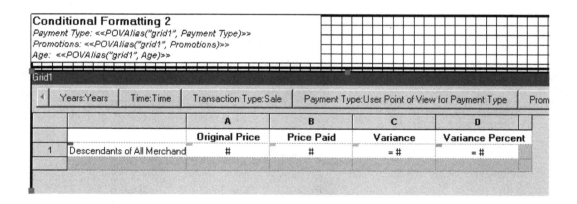

Notice the colors in the upper left-hand corner of each cell. Cells displaying the same color denote that they contain the same conditional formatting configuration. Cells displaying different colors demonstrate that different formatting configurations are applied across the report.

In the example, a new *Variance Percent* column was created in Col D which contains a formula that computes the percentage and the conditional formatting for spotlighting. Opening the conditional format window on the Variance Percent column shows the following six format tabs/conditions.

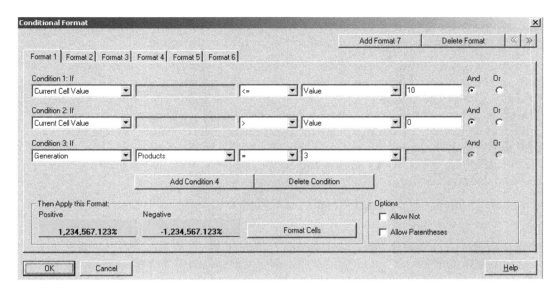

The first question that comes to mind when looking at this example is: *"Why is there a need for six format conditions for three colors?"* The reason is that we want to demonstrate both number formatting and dimension (generation) formatting in this example. In the prior example, the generation 3 Products output row contained a bottom border on the cell as well as underline and bold text. Since spotlighting is now applied, an additional set of formats is required to handle both the dimension and spotlighting formats. Notice Format 1 accommodates both the dimensional formatting and spotlighting conditions for the *green* outcome.

The Format 2 tab displays the same spotlighting conditions as Format 1 but does not include dimensional logic for generation 3.

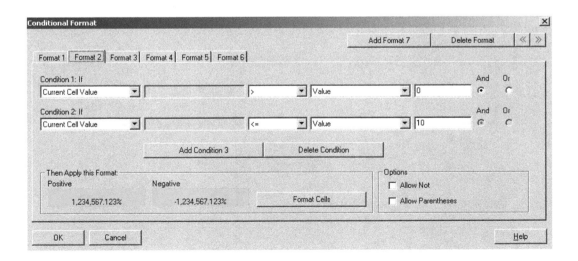

This is a perfect example of where the order of precedence comes into effect; where the order of format tabs is essential to the display returned in the report.

If Format 2 came before Format 1, Format 2 would be satisfied for every condition because it is a superset of the conditions. In this case, the generation 3 specific formatting would be continuously ignored since the first condition is always satisfied. The order of precedence issue could have been mitigated by adding a generation 3 condition with a *Not* operator to make the two sets distinct. However, adding this additional condition requires more maintenance. Utilizing the evaluation order provides the necessary functionality to achieve the desired outcome without the need for additional maintenance.

Continuing with the remaining Format tabs, Format 4 is set up as follows:

Format 6 is set up as follows:

Format 4 and Format 6 display methods for adding color spotlights. Formats 3 and 5 do the same but also contain generation 3 formatting for adding the bold, underline, and bottom border configuration. Running the report displays the following:

Conditional Formatting 2
Payment Type: Payment Type
Promotions: Newspaper Ad
Age: Age

Years: Years Time: Time Transaction Type: Sale Income Level: Income Level Stores: Stores Geography: Geography

	Original Price	Price Paid	Variance	Variance Percent
Digital Cameras	16,196	14,576	1,620	10.000%
Camcorders	30,264	27,238	3,026	10.000%
Photo Printers	17,316	15,584	1,732	10.000%
Digital Cameras/Camcorders	63,776	57,398	6,378	10.000%
Handhelds	0	0	0	0
Memory	36,679	33,011	3,668	10.000%
Other Accessories	87,881	79,092	8,788	10.000%
Handhelds/PDAs	124,560	112,104	12,456	10.000%
Boomboxes	20,330	18,297	2,033	10.000%
Radios	23,147	20,833	2,314	9.997%
Portable Audio	43,477	39,130	4,347	9.998%
Personal Electronics	**231,812**	**208,632**	**23,181**	**10.000%**

In the report output above, some variances show the same values but are in different spotlight colors. The numbers in this example are rounded, with some values falling into the green range (equal to, or below, 10%) and others falling into the yellow range (above 10%). Notice the formatting of the Variance Percent column for the Personal Electronics line. The bold text, underline, and cell bottom border formatting is applied in addition to the spotlighting.

Member Replacement

One unique feature of Financial Reporting is the ability to replace the values of cells. In fact, the use of the **Replacement** feature within conditional formatting allows for specific cell replacements.

In the following example, the Variance % formula row for the generation 3 row is replaced with an N/A. Replacing specific totals or cells in a formula with a blank value or override value is a unique feature that is especially useful with calculations. In some instances, having the ability to blank out a calculation at a particular level is a requirement of the user community and the selective use of this feature is available through conditional formatting.

Chapter 6

This example is similar to the example from the previous section, where the formula for Variance % for any member with a generation of 3 is replaced with a N/A. The following screenshot shows the grid of the third conditional formatting example.

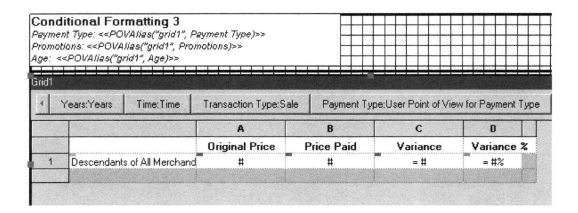

The conditional formatting window for Col D is displayed in the following screenshot.

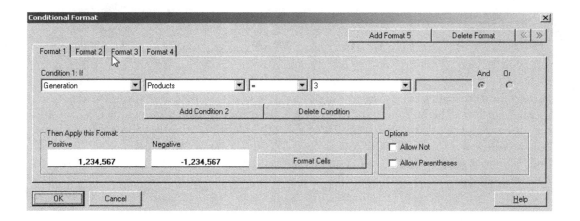

Notice only four formats are used for this example. The first format condition evaluates whether the member returned in the grid is at the 3rd generation of the Products dimension. If the condition is met, the format of the cell is set to bold, underline, and the bottom cell border is applied. Additionally, the Replace tab is configured to display an N/A instead of the value calculated by the report.

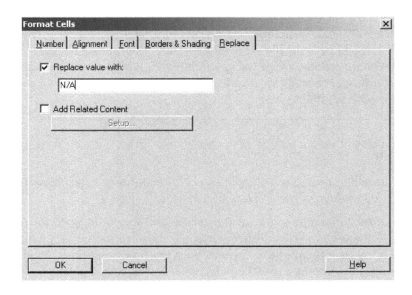

Format tabs 2, 3, and 4 display the spotlighting configuration for the red, yellow, and green conditions. The order of precedence plays into this example as well, where Format 1 contains the dimensional configuration. If the returned member is not a 3rd generation member, the spotlighting configuration is applied. Running the report displays as follows:

Conditional Formatting 3
Payment Type: Payment Type
Promotions: Newspaper Ad
Age: Age

<u>Years: Years</u> <u>Time: Time</u> <u>Transaction Type: Sale</u> <u>Income Level: Income Level</u> <u>Stores: Stores</u> <u>Geography: Geography</u>

	Original Price	Price Paid	Variance	Variance %
Digital Cameras	16,196	14,576	1,620	10%
Camcorders	30,264	27,238	3,026	10%
Photo Printers	17,316	15,584	1,732	10%
Digital Cameras/Camcorders	63,776	57,398	6,378	10%
Handhelds	0	0	0	0%
Memory	36,679	33,011	3,668	10%
Other Accessories	87,881	79,092	8,788	10%
Handhelds/PDAs	124,560	112,104	12,456	10%
Boomboxes	20,330	18,297	2,033	10%
Radios	23,147	20,833	2,314	10%
Portable Audio	43,477	39,130	4,347	10%
Personal Electronics	**231,812**	**208,632**	**23,181**	**N/A**

> Note: The conditional formatting configuration of the Variance % column is simpler than the prior spotlighting example. This is simplified because the generation 3 values do not need the spotlighting conditions since the value is now N/A. Only four format tabs are required, one for the generation 3 settings and one for each spotlight color.

Summary

Conditional formatting provides a number of useful features to enhance report outputs as well as reduce report development and maintenance.

The chapter started with an overview of the conditional formatting interface and examined the formatting controls of the interface for grid formatting. The interface provides the ability to apply multiple formats with multiple conditions, creating the complexity needed to support advanced business requirements. The chapter also introduced the concept of the evaluation order for formatting conditions.

The chapter continued with three examples commonly used in reports. The first example displayed formatting based on a dimensional position, showing how member selection function and formatting can be combined to support unique formatting based on the position of a member in the dimensional hierarchy. The second example was the use of the spotlighting feature in addition to the dimensional position, creating a solid example of order of precedence and the complexity of multiple formats and conditions. The final example displayed the methods for using cell replacement, which is a unique method of removing a value from display using conditional formatting. Each example shows a different capability that can be built upon or modified to support many practical requirements across organizations.

7

Suppression and Conditional Suppression

Multi-dimensional applications have a wide range of data intersections, which grow as the size and number of dimensions in an application increase. Missing data in an application may sound concerning, but missing data is a common and unique feature of these applications. When working with multi-dimensional products, missing data is purely described as an intersection in an application where no stored data exists.

When working with Hyperion products, **Suppression** is commonly utilized to dynamically remove zero, missing, or error intersections from display. Financial Reporting provides the ability to apply basic suppression as well as a more in-depth and complicated method called **Conditional Suppression**. Conditional suppression is a way to conceal row or column data based on conditional logic and values. Both methods play an integral role in developing reports and displaying desired content.

The following content is introduced in this chapter:

- Understanding Basic Suppression
- Understanding Conditional Suppression
- Conditional Suppression Examples

Understanding Basic Suppression

When a grid is added to a report, it is set to show all rows by default to include missing, zero and error values in the returned or calculated results. **Missing** values are defined as an empty intersection or intersection with **no data. Zero** values are where the value 0 is stored at the intersection. **Error values** are commonly associated with formula errors or other complications.

Earlier, in *Chapter 3*, methods were presented to demonstrate replacing missing, zero, and error values with a text character. While using *cell replacement* is a common approach, users may need to remove or suppress records from the report entirely. In this case, **Basic Suppression** is used to facilitate the removal and is set in either the rows, columns, or the grid in its entirety. In the simplest example, highlighting the entire grid in the designer and selecting the Suppression option from the grid properties window brings up the grid suppression settings as shown in the following screenshot.

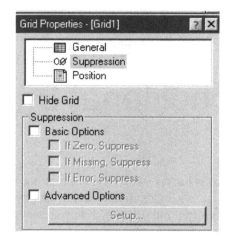

The Basic Options section suppresses dimension values when zero, missing, or error values are returned. Each of the options are turned on by selecting the main checkbox and then by checking each option individually. Basic suppression does not apply to individual cells but rather the rows or columns of the report. If the entire grid is suppressed for all three options, entire rows or columns that do not contain a valid data point are removed from display.

The grid in the following screenshot shows a row with #MISSING and #ERROR when suppression is not applied to the grid.

Years: Years Time: Time Transaction Type: Sale Income Level: Income Level
Stores: Stores Geography: Geography

	Original Price	Price Paid	Variance
Digital Cameras	1,275,216	1,267,367	7,849
Camcorders	2,606,617	2,591,322	15,295
Photo Printers	1,246,060	1,238,122	7,938
Digital Cameras/Camcorders	5,127,893	5,096,812	31,081
Handhelds	#MISSING	#MISSING	#ERROR
Memory	2,455,370	2,437,885	17,485
Other Accessories	6,078,599	6,038,558	40,041
Handhelds/PDAs	8,533,969	8,476,443	57,526

Suppressing the row is achieved by selecting the appropriate row in the grid and applying the supression settings as shown in the following screenshot.

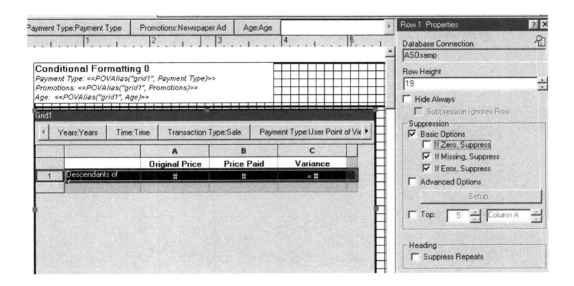

Executing the grid displays as follows:

Years: Years Time: Time Transaction Type: Sale Income Level: Income Level Stores: Stores Geography: Geography			
	Original Price	Price Paid	Variance
Digital Cameras	1,275,216	1,267,367	7,849
Camcorders	2,606,617	2,591,322	15,295
Photo Printers	1,246,060	1,238,122	7,938
Digital Cameras/Camcorders	5,127,893	5,096,812	31,081
Memory	2,455,370	2,437,885	17,485
Other Accessories	6,078,599	6,038,558	40,041
Handhelds/PDAs	8,533,969	8,476,443	57,526
Boomboxes	1,620,347	1,608,859	11,488
Radios	1,559,503	1,549,827	9,676
Portable Audio	3,179,849	3,158,686	21,164

Notice the Handhelds row is no longer displayed on the report during runtime.

Understanding Conditional Suppression

Conditional suppression is a method of using a condition, or conditional logic, to invoke a concealment operation. It works with User Point of View selections, ranges of values, cell values, aliases, attributes, and other features. Once the set condition is satisfied, the column, or row of data where the condition is applied, is omitted from the report at runtime.

Conditional Suppression Interface

Conditional Suppression is accessed through Advanced Options from the grid, row, or column properties.

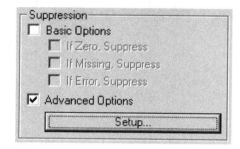

Selecting the checkbox and pressing the Setup button opens the Conditional Suppression window.

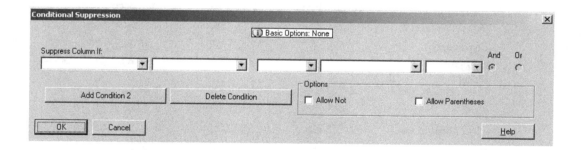

The conditional suppression window has a similar appearance to the conditional format window and allows for the addition of multiple conditions with advanced logic including parentheses, not, and and/or options. The first drop-down box in each condition is used to select the method to act upon and the subsequent boxes update with selectable related information.

Combined Basic and Advanced Suppression Options

The ability to combine basic and conditional suppression options exists. Notice the top of the conditional suppression window in the screenshot below.

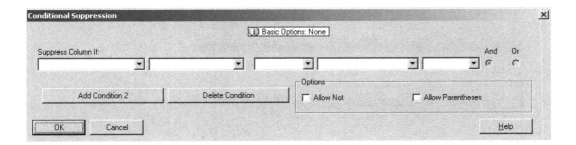

The Basic Options: None label is displayed and denotes that None of the basic suppression options are currently applied. If all of the basic options are turned on, the label at the top of the window updates as shown.

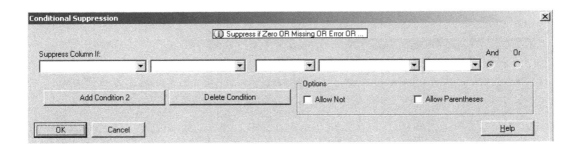

The label is now Suppress if Zero OR Missing OR Error OR... and the basic options are now included in the conditional list. The ability to use both basic and advanced suppression options together removes the need to manually program basic options into the conditional window.

Example 1: Suppressing a Row Based on a Column

The first example demonstrates the method to suppress a row based on a value returned in a column. This suppression operation is commonly used to display rows when a particular cell is accurate or displayed, which in this case is the presence of an accurate variance. The example uses the conditional formatting report from the previous chapter. If the *Variance* column displays *any* of the three conditions (zero, missing, or error) for a data row, the whole row is suppressed in the report. Notice Row 1 in the screenshot below. The basic suppression options are ignored and the advanced suppression option is selected.

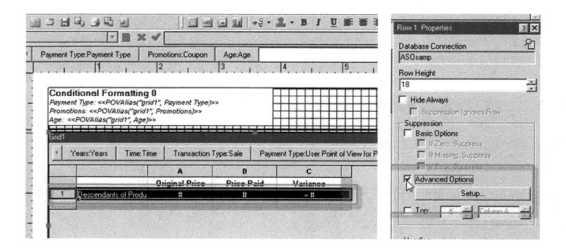

Pressing the Setup button opens the conditional suppression configuration window. In this example, if any one of the three conditions shown below (*Missing* or *No Data*, *Zero*, or *Error*) are experienced in the Variance column (*Col C*), then the row is to be suppressed.

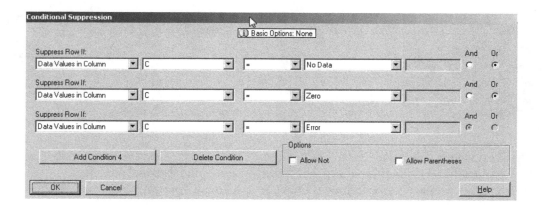

The Data Values in Column condition looks across the data values in the specified column (Col C) in the second dropdown box and evaluates if the value in the column - for each row - is equal to the any of the three conditions (configured by using the Or option between conditions). If any of the conditions are satisfied, the row is suppressed.

The following screenshot shows the grid before applying the settings:

	Original Price	Price Paid	Variance
Digital Cameras	14,744	12,532	2,212
Camcorders	38,214	32,482	5,732
Photo Printers	16,996	14,447	2,549
Digital Cameras/Camcorders	69,954	59,461	10,493
Handhelds	#MISSING	#MISSING	#ERROR
Memory	36,805	31,284	5,521
Other Accessories	86,468	73,499	12,969
Handhelds/PDAs	123,273	104,783	18,490
Boomboxes	25,245	21,459	3,786
Radios	23,048	19,591	3,457
Portable Audio	48,293	41,050	7,243
Personal Electronics	241,519	205,293	36,226
Direct View	#MISSING	#MISSING	#ERROR
Projection TVs	29,120	24,752	4,368

Once conditional suppression settings are applied, the grid displays as follows:

	Original Price	Price Paid	Variance
Digital Cameras	14,744	12,532	2,212
Camcorders	38,214	32,482	5,732
Photo Printers	16,996	14,447	2,549
Digital Cameras/Camcorders	69,954	59,461	10,493
Memory	36,805	31,284	5,521
Other Accessories	86,468	73,499	12,969
Handhelds/PDAs	123,273	104,783	18,490
Boomboxes	25,245	21,459	3,786
Radios	23,048	19,591	3,457
Portable Audio	48,293	41,050	7,243
Personal Electronics	241,519	205,293	36,226
Projection TVs	29,120	24,752	4,368

Note that the rows displaying the #MISSING and #ERROR values are no longer displayed in the grid.

Example 2: Suppression Based on POV Selection

One of the benefits of conditional suppression is the ability to suppress a row or column based on a selection by a user in the **Point of View**. This example continues with an example from previous chapters and shows Merchandise along with Original Price, Price Paid, Variance, and Variance % columns.

Conditional Suppression 1
Payment Type: Payment Type
Promotions: Coupon
Age: Age

Years: Years Time: Time Transaction Type: Sale Income Level: Income Level Stores: Stores Geography: Geography

	Original Price	Price Paid	Variance	Variance Percent
Digital Cameras	14,744	12,532	2,212	15.00%
Camcorders	38,214	32,482	5,732	15.00%
Photo Printers	16,996	14,447	2,549	15.00%
Digital Cameras/Camcorders	69,954	59,461	10,493	15.00%
Handhelds	0	0	0	0
Memory	36,805	31,284	5,521	15.00%
Other Accessories	86,468	73,499	12,969	15.00%
Handhelds/PDAs	123,273	104,783	18,490	15.00%
Boomboxes	25,245	21,459	3,786	15.00%
Radios	23,048	19,591	3,457	15.00%
Portable Audio	48,293	41,050	7,243	15.00%
Personal Electronics	**241,519**	**205,293**	**36,226**	15.00%
Direct View	0	0	0	0
Projection TVs	29,120	24,752	4,368	15.00%

Notice that the Promotions Point of View selection is set to Coupon, which is why the Original Price is different from the Price Paid, and the Variance and Variance Percent columns show the discount that was provided for each product line. If this same report was run with the selection No Promotion, the two Variance columns would show zero and provide a less than desirable display.

Conditional Suppression 1
Payment Type: Payment Type
Promotions: No Promotion
Age: Age

Years: Years Time: Time Transaction Type: Sale Income Level: Income Level Stores: Stores Geography: Geography

	Original Price	Price Paid	Variance	Variance Percent
Digital Cameras	1,224,188	1,224,188	0	0
Camcorders	2,505,458	2,505,458	0	0
Photo Printers	1,193,464	1,193,464	0	0
Digital Cameras/Camcorders	4,923,110	4,923,110	0	0
Handhelds	0	0	0	0
Memory	2,340,404	2,340,404	0	0
Other Accessories	5,812,833	5,812,833	0	0
Handhelds/PDAs	8,153,237	8,153,237	0	0
Boomboxes	1,546,430	1,546,430	0	0
Radios	1,493,783	1,493,783	0	0
Portable Audio	3,040,213	3,040,213	0	0
Personal Electronics	**16,116,559**	**16,116,559**	**0**	0
Direct View	0	0	0	0
Projection TVs	1,802,680	1,802,680	0	0

In this example, there is a need to remove the Variance and Variance Percent columns through the use of conditional suppression. In this case, the two columns are selected and Advanced Options are set as shown.

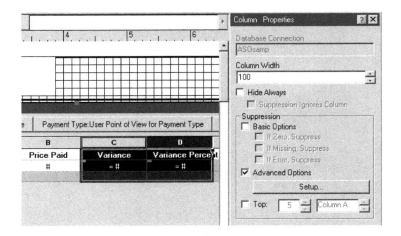

Conditional suppression is configured to suppress the column if the Member Name for the POV selection - for the Promotions dimension - is No Promotion. The following

screenshot shows the configuration of the conditional suppression window for the condition.

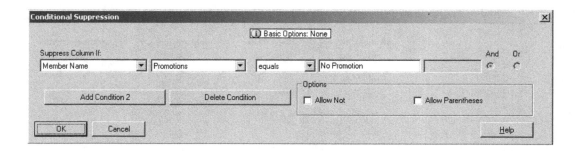

Notice that the configuration window does not reference the POV but rather the member name equaling a value. The Member Name operation is selected in the first drop-down, the Promotions dimension is selected in the second drop-down, the equals operator in the third drop-down, and the text No Promotion is entered into the textbox. Running the report displays values for the two variance columns when all selections for the Promotions dimension are selected *except* for the No Promotion member. When the report is run for the *No Promotion* member, the report displays as follows:

Conditional Suppression 1
Payment Type: Payment Type
Promotions: No Promotion
Age: Age

Years: Years Time: Time Transaction Type: Sale Income Level:
Income Level Stores: Stores Geography: Geography

	Original Price	Price Paid
Digital Cameras	1,224,188	1,224,188
Camcorders	2,505,458	2,505,458
Photo Printers	1,193,464	1,193,464
Digital Cameras/Camcorders	4,923,110	4,923,110
Handhelds	0	0
Memory	2,340,404	2,340,404
Other Accessories	5,812,833	5,812,833
Handhelds/PDAs	8,153,237	8,153,237
Boomboxes	1,546,430	1,546,430
Radios	1,493,783	1,493,783
Portable Audio	3,040,213	3,040,213
Personal Electronics	**16,116,559**	**16,116,559**
Direct View	0	0
Projection TVs	1,802,680	1,802,680
Flat Panel	1,444,245	1,444,245
HDTV	5,124,188	5,124,188

Example 3: Suppression Based on a Value Range

Conditional suppression may be utilized to suppress data based on a range of values. In the following example, the desire is to supress any row of data with a Variance column of less than 40,000. This approach is commonly used to look through data sets and identify outliers, ranges, and particular values of interest. The following screenshot shows the example grid without applying the suppression condition.

Years: Years Time: Time Transaction Type: Sale Income Level: Income Level Stores: Stores
Geography: Geography

	Original Price	Price Paid	Variance
Digital Cameras	1,275,216	1,267,367	7,849
Camcorders	2,606,617	2,591,322	15,295
Photo Printers	1,246,060	1,238,122	7,938
Digital Cameras/Camcorders	5,127,893	5,096,812	31,081
Memory	2,455,370	2,437,885	17,485
Other Accessories	6,078,599	6,038,558	40,041
Handhelds/PDAs	8,533,969	8,476,443	57,526
Boomboxes	1,620,347	1,608,859	11,488
Radios	1,559,503	1,549,827	9,676
Portable Audio	3,179,849	3,158,686	21,164
Personal Electronics	**16,841,711**	**16,731,941**	**109,771**
Projection TVs	1,907,000	1,892,488	14,512
Flat Panel	1,508,045	1,497,882	10,163
HDTV	5,390,138	5,350,020	40,117
Stands	1,732,815	1,721,876	10,939
Televisions	10,537,998	10,462,266	75,731
Home Theater	1,420,115	1,410,569	9,546
Digital Recorders	818,360	812,788	5,572
DVD	2,036,980	2,023,494	13,486
Home Audio/Video	4,275,455	4,246,851	28,603
Home Entertainment	**14,813,452**	**14,709,117**	**104,335**

Conditional suppression is subsequently applied using the Data Values in Column condition, and basic options must be turned on to include the suppression of missing and error values. The following screenshot shows the configuration of the advanced condition.

Conditional Suppression

Suppress if Missing OR Error OR ...

Suppress Row If:

| Data Values in Column ▼ | C | ▼ | <= | ▼ | Value | ▼ | 40000 | And ⊙ | Or ○ |

Add Condition 2   Delete Condition

Options
☐ Allow Not   ☐ Allow Parentheses

OK   Cancel   Help

The report now displays as follows:

Years: Years Time: Time Transaction Type: Sale Income Level: Income Level Stores: Stores Geography: Geography

	Original Price	Price Paid	Variance
Other Accessories	6,078,599	6,038,558	40,041
Handhelds/PDAs	8,533,969	8,476,443	57,526
Personal Electronics	**16,841,711**	**16,731,941**	**109,771**
HDTV	5,390,138	5,350,020	40,117
Televisions	10,537,998	10,462,266	75,731
Home Entertainment	**14,813,452**	**14,709,117**	**104,335**

Example 4: Suppression of a Generation or Level

Conditional suppression can be used to suppress a set of values from a grid based on a dimension Level or Generation. In the following example, the grid contains one row used to generate all of the Descendants of All Merchandise in the Product dimension.

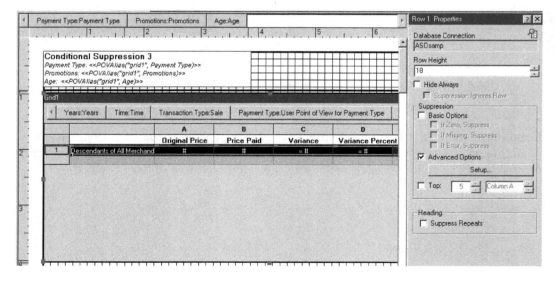

The following screenshot shows the example grid without applying the suppression condition.

Years: Years Time: Time Transaction Type: Sale Income Level: Income Level Stores: Store Geography			
	Original Price	Price Paid	Variance
Digital Cameras	1,275,216	1,267,367	7,849
Camcorders	2,606,617	2,591,322	15,295
Photo Printers	1,246,060	1,238,122	7,938
Digital Cameras/Camcorders	5,127,893	5,096,812	31,081
Handhelds	0	0	0
Memory	2,455,370	2,437,885	17,485
Other Accessories	6,078,599	6,038,558	40,041
Handhelds/PDAs	8,533,969	8,476,443	57,526
Boomboxes	1,620,347	1,608,859	11,488
Radios	1,559,503	1,549,827	9,676
Portable Audio	3,179,849	3,158,686	21,164
Personal Electronics	**16,841,711**	**16,731,941**	**109,771**
Direct View	0	0	0
Projection TVs	1,907,000	1,892,488	14,512

Conditional formatting is used in the grid to indent each level based on the position in the hierarchy, where members such as Digital Cameras, Camcorders, Photo Printers, Handhelds, etc. are *Level 0* members. In this suppression example, all the *Level 0* members from the Product dimension are suppressed– leaving only the upper-level values.

The conditional suppression interface is set on the first row of the report and configured to use the Level condition. The Products dimension is selected and the grid is set to suppress rows set equal to level 0 as shown.

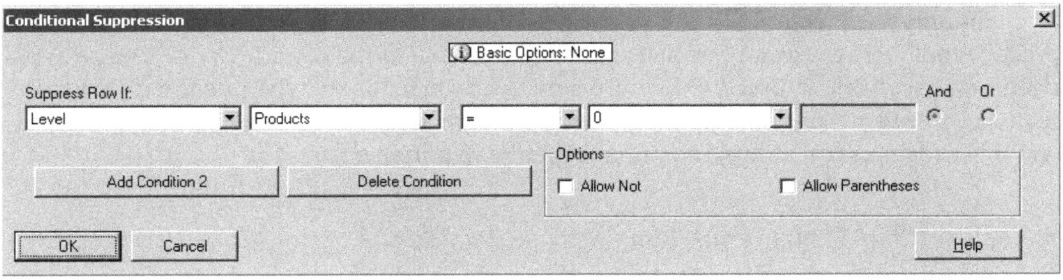

127

Notice the suppressed report shows a much smaller set of data, which includes Level 1 members (and above) in the hierarchy.

Years: Years Time: Time Transaction Type: Sale Income Level: Income Level Stores: Store Geography	Original Price	Price Paid	Variance
Digital Cameras/Camcorders	5,127,893	5,096,812	31,081
Handhelds/PDAs	8,533,969	8,476,443	57,526
Portable Audio	3,179,849	3,158,686	21,164
Personal Electronics	**16,841,711**	**16,731,941**	**109,771**
Televisions	10,537,998	10,462,266	75,731
Home Audio/Video	4,275,455	4,246,851	28,603
Home Entertainment	**14,813,452**	**14,709,117**	**104,335**
Systems	4,166,050	4,138,863	27,188
Computers and Peripherals	4,166,050	4,138,863	27,188
Other	**4,166,050**	**4,138,863**	**27,188**

Summary

Suppression is one of the most commonly used features of Financial Reporting and nearly all developed grids are configured with a form of suppression. While the need to remove zero and missing values from display is the primary use, the ability to apply suppression using a set of conditions and values provides unrelenting flexibility to generate a desired display.

The chapter began with an overview of suppression and the use of basic suppression options. Basic suppression options provide an easy way to suppress commonly experienced zero, missing, and error values without the need for additional configuration. The chapter continued with an introduction to conditional suppression, which is the advanced suppression method utilized to suppress grid rows or columns based on custom conditions and values. With a wide variety of conditional suppression techniques available, the chapter discussed the interface and then provided four examples of commonly used techniques. The examples demonstrate common approaches used in practice today. These examples just scratch the surface of the complexity of suppression conditions available to users, where users are recommended to experiment with the tool features. *Chapter 8* provides additional examples of advanced conditional suppression and other features to facilitate common business requirements.

8

Advanced Techniques

Earlier chapters in the book have focused on learning individual techniques in Financial Reporting, providing a framework to facilitate successful report building. This chapter focuses on methods that can be used to solve a set of common but complex business scenarios, providing insight into combinations of techniques that satisfy elaborate requirements. These scenarios range from combining data from multiple grids into a single grid, generating a grid that displays the top ranked items in a desired data set, creating a rolling forecast using formulas and suppression, supporting external values in functions, and integrating more than one application through dimension mapping.

The following content is introduced in this chapter:

- Scenario 1: Integrating Multiple Grids with Formulas
- Scenario 2: Custom Text and Values on Heading Labels
- Scenario 3: Combining Actual & Budget (Rolling Forecast)
- Scenario 4: Storing Constants for use in Expressions
- Scenario 5: The Top 5
- Scenario 6: One Grid, Multiple Data Sources

Scenario 1: Integrating Multiple Grids with Formulas

With many reports, requested data cannot be queried using a single grid. In many cases, values are stored in different areas of the application, requiring techniques that query the supplemental data before integrating it into the main grid for display. The Point of View for the main and supplemental data sets commonly differ, requiring the use of multiple grids to query specific values and the use of formulas to integrate them into the main grid.

Using an example referenced throughout the book, two grids are added to the report and the data from the second grid is integrated into the first grid using a cell reference. This example is very simple and is specifically used to demonstrate multi-grid functionality. In the example below, a new formula column is added to the end of Grid 1.

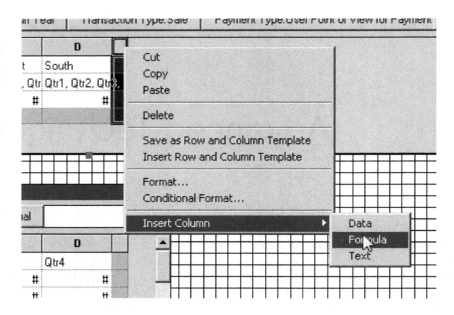

A new formula column is added to pull the Qtr4 East values from Grid 2 into Grid 1 through the use of column references. The custom column heading East is added to the formula column as shown below.

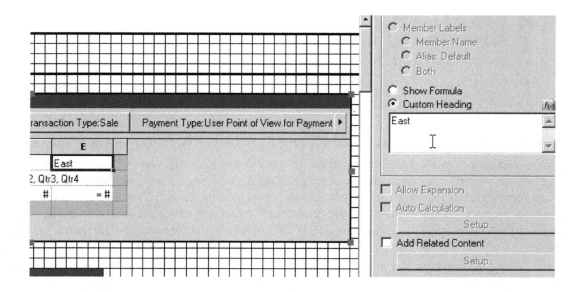

Similarly, Qtr4 was added for the second header row as shown.

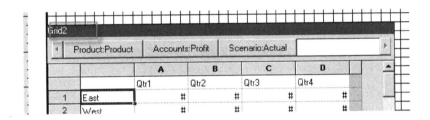

Grid 2 was added to the report below Grid 1 and displays geographical data by individual quarter.

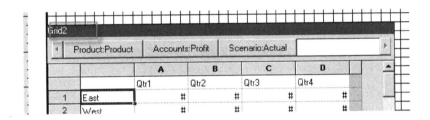

In this example, the data in Grid 2 → Row 1 → Column D is referenced in Grid 1 using a formula. The formula is added by typing on Grid 1 → Row 1 → Column E and adding the syntax to pull from the cell in Grid 2. The syntax for pulling a specific cell is Grid2.[D,1], where the Grid Name must be used to specify the external grid. The screenshot below shows the configuration of the formula cell. After the formula is typed into the formula bar, the green checkbox is selected to apply the formula to the cell.

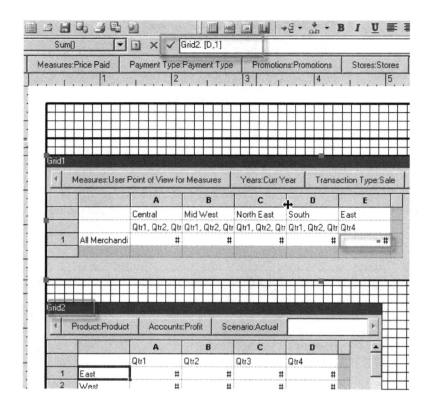

With the formula cell configured, the data from Grid 2 now appears in the specific cell in Grid 1. At this time, Grid 2 still appears when the report is run. However, Financial Reporting allows for the hiding of Grid 2 while still allowing the reference in Grid 1. Grid 2 is hidden by selecting Grid 2 and the Hide Grid checkbox on the grid properties window as shown in the following screenshot.

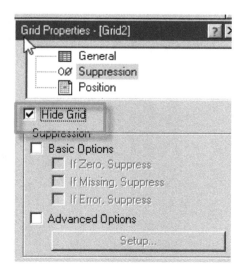

Executing the report shows Grid 1 with the desired results and a hidden second grid:

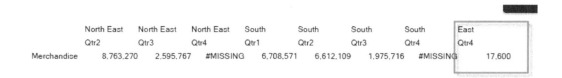

	North East Qtr2	North East Qtr3	North East Qtr4	South Qtr1	South Qtr2	South Qtr3	South Qtr4	East Qtr4
Merchandise	8,763,270	2,595,767	#MISSING	6,708,571	6,612,109	1,975,716	#MISSING	17,600

> Note: Report performance may degrade with the additional complexity of multiple grids. As additional grids are added and complexity increased, report runtime increases. It is important to identify an efficient approach and test performance throughout the development process.

Scenario 2: Custom Text and Values on Heading Labels

The use of text functions provides a means to customize the text labels on a report. Users may require a report to contain specific *data* values from the application along with text in column labels to enhance the display. Using the same report from Scenario 1, the data in Grid 2 for the East intersection is pulled and displayed in the row *label* for Row 1. Selecting the row label in Row 1 for Merchandise opens the Heading Row Properties as shown in the following screenshot. Notice the function button displayed to the right of the Custom Heading radio button.

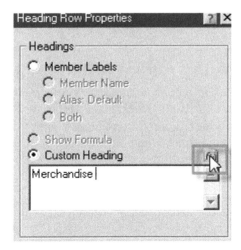

After selecting the function button, the Insert Function window appears. Functions may be typed or selected. In this example, both the MemberAlias and GetCell functions are used to pull the alias of the member as well as the specific cell value. Both functions may be combined with additional text to display the desired label. The heading for the row is configured with the text Merchandise and the two functions as displayed in the following screenshot.

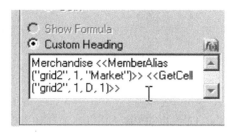

Notice the MemberAlias function references the Alias of the Market dimension for the values in Row 1 of the second grid. Additionally, the GetCell function pulls data from the cell [D,1] of the second grid.

Running the report displays the dynamic alias East along with the data value 17.600 in the row label as shown in the following screenshot.

Scenario 3: Combining Actual & Budget (Rolling Forecast)

Across businesses, the ability to combine actual performance with a forecast or budget scenario is a common operation. While forecasts in Hyperion Planning are commonly completed through using a standard copy-then-forecast approach, this approach demonstrates the combination of more than one scenario in a single row (without copying the data), displaying the rolling forecast values based on the time period selected in the report.

This example uses a newly configured grid and report to demonstrate the approach. The following screenshot shows the example grid with the Measures in the rows and the Year (Period) and Scenario in the columns. *In this sample Essbase application, the Year dimension contains all of the months (Jan – Dec).*

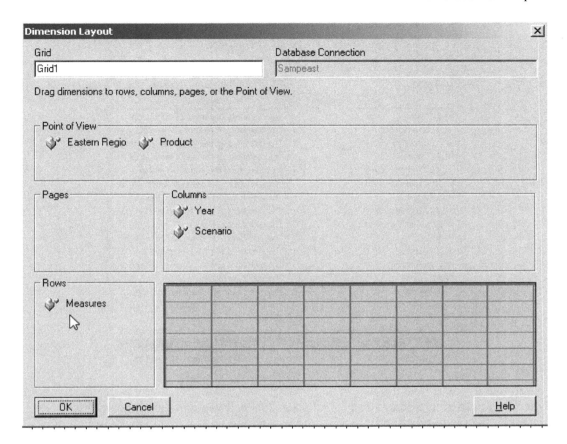

Additionally, the Children of Profit selection was configured for the Measures dimension as shown in the following screenshot.

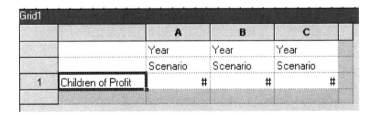

Continuing with the example, Column A is set to Actual, and the Year dimension is configured using a Range function as demonstrated below.

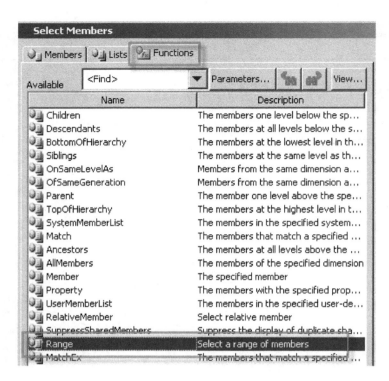

The Range function displays a set of columns for each value in the range. In this example, the range function starts with the first period Jan and continues through the Current Point of View for Year.

Note: A substitution variable is also commonly used with similar examples, allowing the administrator to control the current period for display across a set of reports.

The configured Range function is displayed as follows:

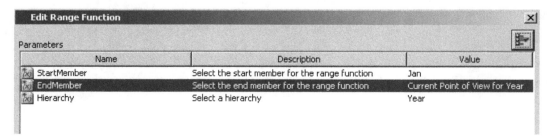

The next step in the example is to configure the range of values for the Budget member for Column B. After selecting the Budget member, the range for Years is configured. Since the column needs to show the Budget for the periods *after* the Current Point of View, a **RelativeMember** function is used inside the Range function in the configuration for the StartMember as shown.

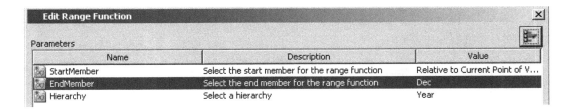

The RelativeMember function provides the ability to derive a member based on its relationship with another member. In this example, the time period is going to be shifted forward one member from the selected member in the Current Point of View. Setting the RelativeMember function is completed by selecting the Functions tab when selecting the StartMember value as shown in the following screenshot.

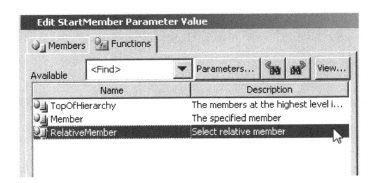

After selecting the RelativeMember function, the configuration window displays as follows:

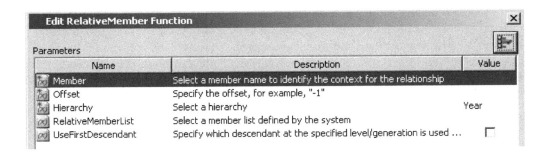

The Member is set to the Current Point of View for the Year dimension. Once the member is set, the next step is to set the Offset. The offset is set to 1 to shift the Current Point of View for the year forward *one* period. The following screenshot shows the fully configured RelativeMember function.

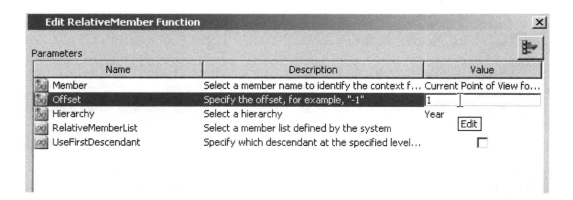

Once the function is accepted, the EndMember for the range is set to Dec to complete the range configuration for the Year dimension of Column B as shown below.

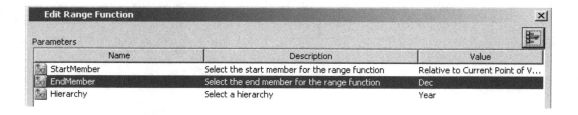

At this point, the configuration works great for all values except for when the current point of view is Dec. When Dec is selected as the current point of view, the Actual range displays from Jan → Dec. However, the Budget range also displays for Jan → Dec, due to the RelativeMember function and the offset utilized. When Dec is selected, the StartMonth for the range in the budget is shifted from Dec to Jan (one place forward). Therefore, Jan → Dec displays for both Budget and Actual, displaying 24 columns.

When situations occur where a non-desired output is displayed, conditional suppression is utilized to hide the errant output. To complete the conditional suppression, a third column is used to support the conditional statement. Column C is configured to Budget for the Scenario and Current Point of View for Year. Note that no range was used in this example, just the Current Point of View. Column C is then hidden and then the Advanced (Conditional) Suppression is configured.

Note: This conditional suppression technique can be completed a few different ways, and the use of a third column is used to demonstrate approaches for using hidden columns for the purposes of suppression.

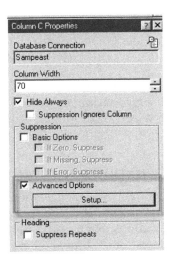

After configuring the conditional suppression window, Column C is suppressed if the Member Name of the Year dimension is set to Dec as shown in the following screenshot.

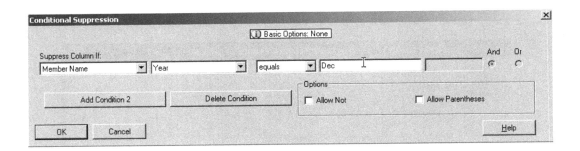

After completing the suppression on Column C, conditional suppression is also applied to Column B. The conditional suppression logic in this column references the hidden Column C and is suppressed only when Column C is suppressed. The appropriate setting for this configuration is shown in the conditional suppression window.

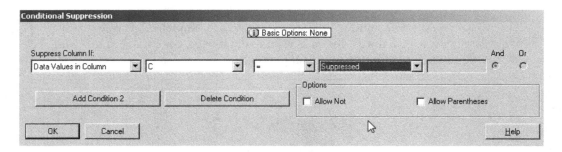

Once complete, the suppression logic mitigates any issue when Dec is selected in the point of view. The report now displays accurately for any period selection, where Actuals are displayed through the month selected and Budget is displayed for each month after the selection through Dec.

Scenario 4: Storing Constants for use in Expressions

When working with reporting requirements that contain calculations, there may be a need to use constants or values not stored inside the application in a report. Constants can be embedded directly into functions, but it is also useful to use a custom grid populated with the desired constants for visibility and easy updating.

Using a constant in an expression requires the use of the `Eval()` function. For example, formulas commonly require the use of subtraction by the value 1 to inverse percentages `(([A]-[B])/[C])-1`. On the surface, the formula appears to be a simple expression. However, the following error message occurs when attempting to evaluate this formula in Financial Reporting:

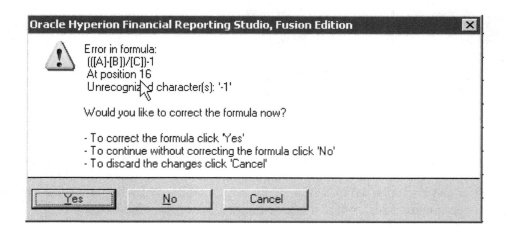

The error occurs to the unidentified constant value at the end of the expression. In Financial Reporting, all constants need to be wrapped with the `Eval()` function to have their values evaluated correctly. The function evaluates correctly when the following syntax is entered: `((([A]-[B])/[C])-Eval(1)`

Additionally, a supplemental grid or formula column can be used to store the constant values hidden from view during display. Using the above example, the insertion of a formula column and addition of a constant of 1 into the function will populate a column with the constant value.

Note: Do not use bracket symbols around the 1 as this would instead tell the formula to use Row 1 instead of the constant value 1. Also note that the Eval() function is not required in the formula when it is not involved in a calculation.

Now the formula for the calculation can reference the column instead of the individual value and serves as an easy option to view constant values and update calculations: `((([A]-[B])/[C])-[D]`.

Scenario 5: The Top 5

The concept of a **Top 5**, Bottom 5, or any subset of ranked values is a common business requirement. Whether the requirement is to show the top five cities, products, programs, or businesses, organizations commonly use top and bottom segmentation to subset the top performers or areas requiring attention.

In this *Top 5* example, the top five products are displayed using the Price Paid as the selection criterion. Utilizing a report from earlier in the book, a new column is added to the grid as shown in the following screenshot.

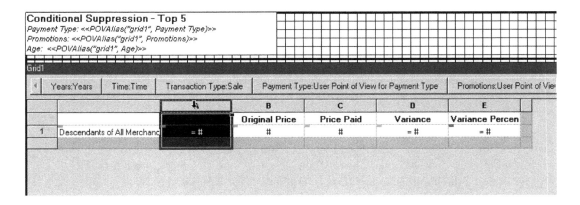

The first step in creating the Top 5 segmentation is to create a column that ranks the values. The **Rank** function is used to rank the values in Column C with the argument Descending to have the highest price paid set to the rank of 1: `Rank([C], Descending)`.

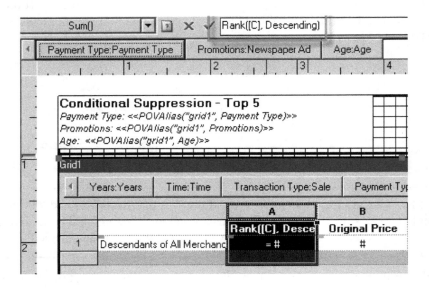

Running the report displays the new rank column with the numerical ranking values as shown below.

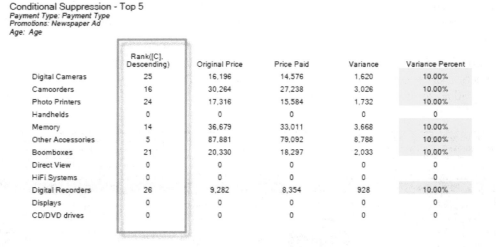

Conditional Suppression - Top 5
Payment Type: Payment Type
Promotions: Newspaper Ad
Age: Age

	Rank([C], Descending)	Original Price	Price Paid	Variance	Variance Percent
Digital Cameras	25	16,196	14,576	1,620	10.00%
Camcorders	16	30,264	27,238	3,026	10.00%
Photo Printers	24	17,316	15,584	1,732	10.00%
Handhelds	0	0	0	0	0
Memory	14	36,679	33,011	3,668	10.00%
Other Accessories	5	87,881	79,092	8,788	10.00%
Boomboxes	21	20,330	18,297	2,033	10.00%
Direct View	0	0	0	0	0
HiFi Systems	0	0	0	0	0
Digital Recorders	26	9,282	8,354	928	10.00%
Displays	0	0	0	0	0
CD/DVD drives	0	0	0	0	0

The next step is to apply conditional suppression to the column and limit the values returned to only display rank values of 5 or less (i.e. our Top 5 requirement). The application of the suppression criteria to Column A is displayed below.

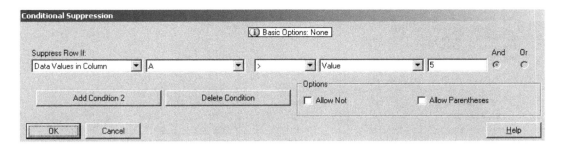

> Note: The suppression criteria and ranking argument can be adjusted to show the desired number of top or bottom items.

Once the condition is applied to the grid and the report is run, the report displays as follows:

Conditional Suppression - Top 5
Payment Type: Payment Type
Promotions: Newspaper Ad
Age: Age

	Rank([C], Descending)	Original Price	Price Paid	Variance	Variance Percent
Handhelds	0	0	0	0	0
Other Accessories	5	87,881	79,092	8,788	10.00%
Handhelds/PDAs	4	124,560	112,104	12,456	10.00%
Personal Electronics	1	231,812	208,632	23,181	10.00%
Direct View	0	0	0	0	0
Televisions	3	178,485	160,637	17,849	10.00%
HiFi Systems	0	0	0	0	0
Home Entertainment	2	228,673	205,806	22,867	10.00%
Displays	0	0	0	0	0
CD/DVD drives	0	0	0	0	0

There are a few issues that still need to be addressed at this point. First, zero and missing values are still being displayed in the report. Setting the Basic Suppression settings on Row 1 to suppress zero, missing, and error values will remove them from display. After applying the additional suppression conditions, the report displays as follows:

Conditional Suppression - Top 5
Payment Type: Payment Type
Promotions: Newspaper Ad
Age: Age

	Rank([C], Descending)	Original Price	Price Paid	Variance	Variance Percent
Other Accessories	5	87,881	79,092	8,788	10.00%
Handhelds/PDAs	4	124,560	112,104	12,456	10.00%
Personal Electronics	1	231,812	208,632	23,181	10.00%
Televisions	3	178,485	160,637	17,849	10.00%
Home Entertainment	2	228,673	205,806	22,867	10.00%

In this example, the Descendants member selection function was used on Row 1 to demonstrate what happens when suppression settings are applied to a dynamic set of values with multiple hierarchy levels. Notice the Rank function takes into account not just the Level 0 members, but also the parent members. There are a few different methods for handling this issue, but one of the easiest is to edit the member selection criteria and add a Level 0 list condition to only show Level 0 members.

To only show the bottom level members for the products hierarchy, two things are needed. The member selection of All Merchandise needs to be edited to include the Lev0,Products list. Secondly, the advanced options must also be edited to ensure the operator applied is And between both member selection criteria.

Executing the report again shows the following output:

Conditional Suppression - Top 5
Payment Type: Payment Type
Promotions: Newspaper Ad
Age: Age

	Rank([C], Descending)	Original Price	Price Paid	Variance	Variance Percent
Memory	4	36,679	33,011	3,668	10.00%
Other Accessories	1	87,881	79,092	8,788	10.00%
Projection TVs	3	48,960	44,064	4,896	10.00%
HDTV	2	87,225	78,503	8,723	10.00%
Desktops	5	33,790	30,411	3,379	10.00%

The output looks better but the ordering of Price Paid is not sorted. Sorting is completed by selecting the entire grid, checking the Sort checkbox, and selecting the Setup button as shown in the following screenshots.

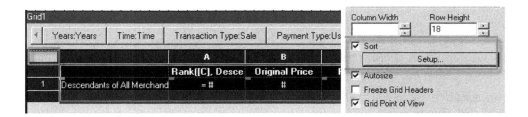

The Sort window opens and is configured, as shown below, to sort the ranked information in Column C in descending order as shown in the following screenshot.

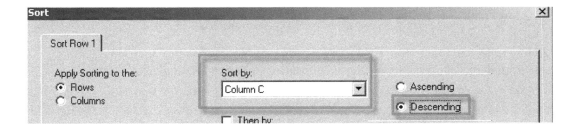

The last step after completing the sorting is to hide the Rank column from display. Once complete, executing the report displays as follows:

Conditional Suppression - Top 5
Payment Type: Payment Type
Promotions: Newspaper Ad
Age: Age

	Original Price	Price Paid	Variance	Variance Percent
Other Accessories	87,881	79,092	8,788	10.00%
HDTV	87,225	78,503	8,723	10.00%
Projection TVs	48,960	44,064	4,896	10.00%
Memory	36,679	33,011	3,668	10.00%
Desktops	33,790	30,411	3,379	10.00%

Notice that the top five Level 0 members are now sorted correctly. Indenting is still applied due to conditional formatting being applied to the grid in an earlier example. This indenting can remain or be removed based on user preferences.

Scenario 6: One Grid, Multiple Data Sources

In some situations, there might be a business need for a Financial Report to pull data from more than one data source. One approach demonstrated earlier is to create a new grid and then link the grids together using formulas. However, there is an additional approach that can be used to switch columns or rows in the report from the main database connection to another connection and perform dimension mapping. This approach is very useful when dealing with cubes that split information across fiscal years, where the cubes are similar enough in dimension configuration to support the mapping.

The approach to switching the connection is fairly simple but it can only be applied to an entire *Data* column or row. After selecting the column or row, select the magnifying glass icon in the database connection section of the column properties window as shown in the following screenshot.

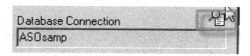

Selecting the icon opens the database connection selection window as shown next.

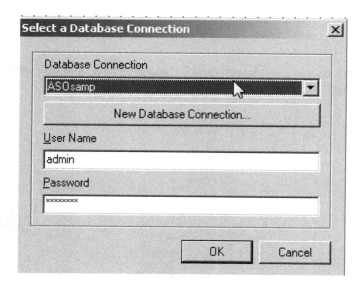

Once the new database connection is selected, the following window appears to map the dimensions.

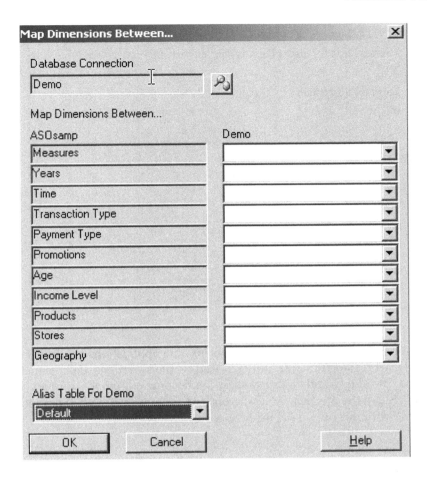

If a corresponding dimension does not map, it can be left blank. After the application dimensions are mapped, selecting the OK button populates the grid with more than one Point of View as shown in the following screenshot.

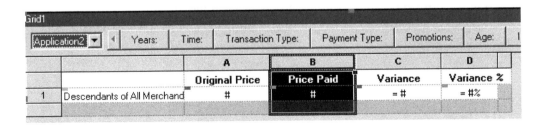

The drop-down box toggles between the two Points of View in the grid, and the newly added data source connection Point of View requires configuration. When the report is run, the User Point of View for each application is displayed as shown in the following screenshot.

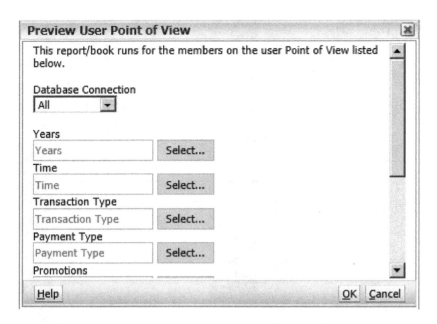

Notice that the Point of View can be selected for both applications combined or for each one individually by using the drop-down. Based on the selections, data is queried and combined into the single grid. This example can become extremely complex with the options available in the product. Trial and error is commonly the best approach to use when working with this option to ensure success.

Summary

Financial Reporting business requirements range from simple to complex. This chapter focused on advanced techniques that are built on the content presented in the previous chapters of the book to illustrate solutions to common business requirements. The chapter addresses multiple grid integration, ranking and suppression to support the concept of a Top 5, expressions and constants, and methods that support rolling forecasting requirements. Each example provides a technique or combination of techniques that can be used to satisfy similar requirements or adapted to satisfy complimentary needs.

9

Report Templates and Text Label Functions

A major benefit of Financial Reporting is the ability to create nicely formatted reports where the on screen version can be easily printed. Many organizations take advantage of the ability to create a standard Financial Reporting template to display a consistent layout for corporate reporting, and these corporate templates commonly include a corporate logo, fonts, and text labels for report titles and specific company markings.

Financial Reporting contains functions to automatically derive page numbers, the report name, the report path, the user who ran the report, user selections, and many other valuable fields. This chapter demonstrates the steps needed to build a nicely formatted corporate template with insight into using text label functions to derive content.

The following content is introduced in this chapter:

- Page Setup
- Headers & Footers
- Images
- Member Functions
- Saving Objects
- General Best Practices for Templates

Setting the Page Size and Margins

The first step in formatting a report is the identification of the page size and layout needed to best accommodate the content. Report developers commonly try to maximize the real estate of the report for printing by using the **Page Setup** menu to configure the page size of the report. The most common setting is the Letter page size and reports are typically developed using a landscape layout. However, reports developed purely for on-screen display can have any desired display size.

The page size is edited by opening the Page Setup window from the File menu as shown in the following screenshot.

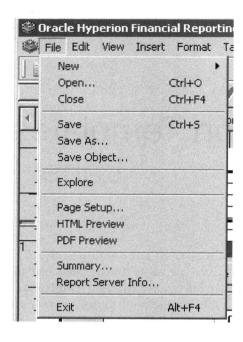

The Page Setup window contains options for editing the page, margins, and Workspace size as shown.

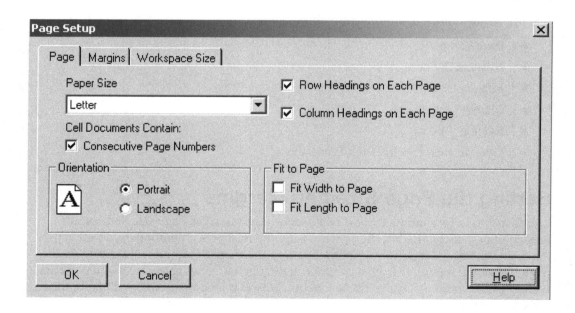

The Page tab is used to set the paper size, orientation, and fit configuration. The paper size drop-down provides the various options available. If a custom size is desired for the report, the Workspace Size tab lets users override the page settings and set a custom height and width to a report. To force the override, click the Use a Custom Workspace Size checkbox and then enter the desired size in inches.

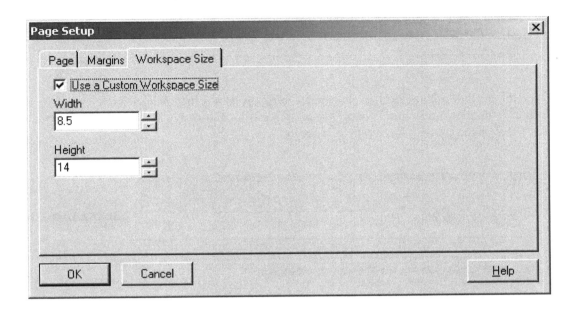

Once the page layout is set to the desired size and orientation, the default margin configuration can be changed. The Margins tab on the page setup window displays four text boxes for changing each margin setting.

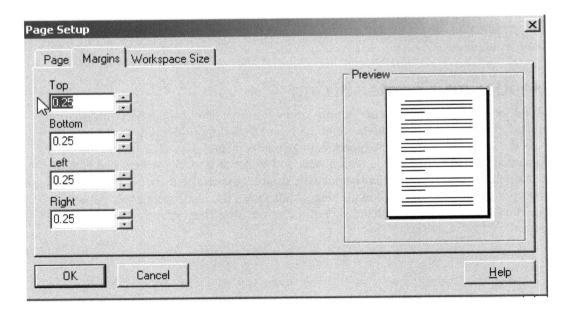

> Note: Resizing the margins to a size smaller than your printer can handle causes the content in the printout to be trimmed around the margin. Make sure to test the print area if editing the margins at less than the default .25 sizing. Adjusting the margins at a later date may take up significantly more development time than testing the print view upon initial formatting.

Once the desired page setup is configured, the report shows the changes to the page layout in the report designer. The following screenshot shows a sample grid for a report in a letter page size with landscape orientation.

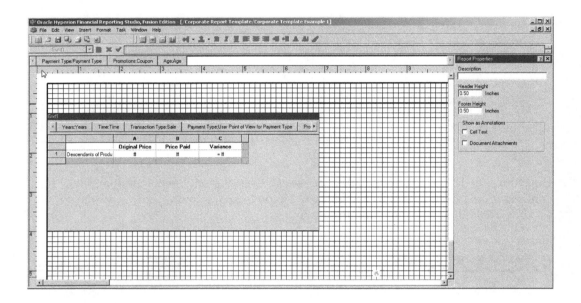

Header and Footer Sizing

Headers and **Footers** are static sections of a report that display summary information and commonly include metadata about the report including title, point of view prompt selections, report runtime, file location, page numbers, and the user who ran the report. Financial Reporting sets the default header and footer area to .50 inches. The default header size is typically smaller than usually desired, especially if user POV selections are shown in the header. The following screenshot shows the report properties window, which is shown on the right-hand side of the screen when the report is the selected object.

The header and footer height may be edited by changing the number of inches in the properties window or by clicking and moving the green icon on the vertical ruler directly across from the header or footer separator line on the report. The ruler object is highlighted in the following screenshot.

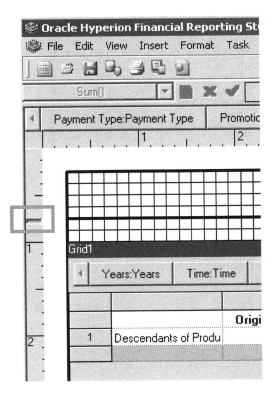

> Note: In the screenshot above, the grid object must be moved lower on the page if the header is larger than the allotted space between the grid and the top of the report. Resizing the header border stops at the first object in the body and does not dynamically move the objects in the body.

Header Content

The headers of reports commonly contain a report title, logo, and information about report selections. In the following example, the header section is built with a report title, company logo, and the User Point of View selections for the report. It is especially important to display the selections made by the user in the report to provide traceability with regard to the filters and numbers generated. If the report does not display the user selections in a viewable area, consumers of the report may misinterpret the metrics produced. The following screenshot shows the report prior to the addition of header content with the page layout and header margin size configured.

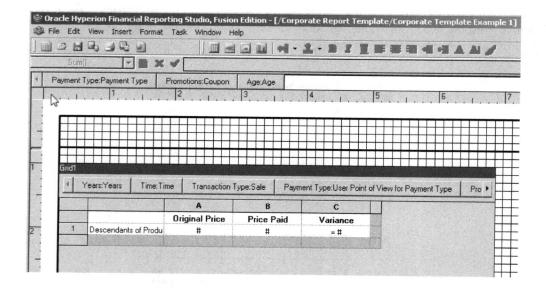

Adding a Report Logo

Images have a dramatic impact on the aesthetics of a report. An image is added to the report by selecting the Image item from the Insert menu as shown in the following screenshot.

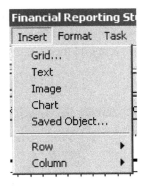

Once the Image menu item is selected, the Financial Reporting Studio interface allows the user to draw the image onto the report. Many organizations choose to add a logo to the right-hand side of the screen. Multiple logos and images can be added to the report as desired. After drawing the image on the right-hand side of the header and releasing the mouse, the image selection window appears as shown in the following screenshot.

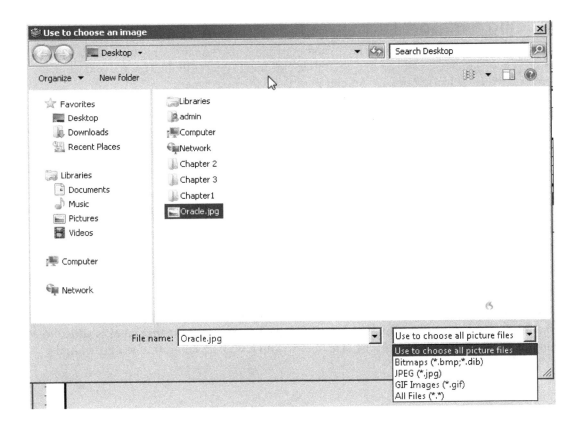

Notice in the screenshot above that the only supported images are Bitmap, JPEG, and GIF images. The example in this book uses the Oracle logo as the logo for the report. Upon selecting the Oracle logo, the image is nicely displayed in the location where the image was drawn.

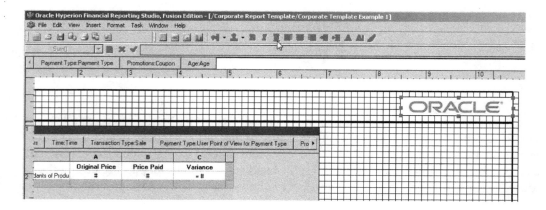

Adding a Report Title

Report titles are commonly displayed and configured as dynamic or static based on preference. Titles are created through the use of **Text** objects in the report. Text objects are created by selecting the Text menu item from the Insert menu.

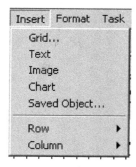

Similar to the image object, selecting the text menu item brings up the drawing icon in the Studio for drawing the text label box onto the report. Once the text label is added to the report, the label appears in the size drawn with a white background as shown in the following screenshot.

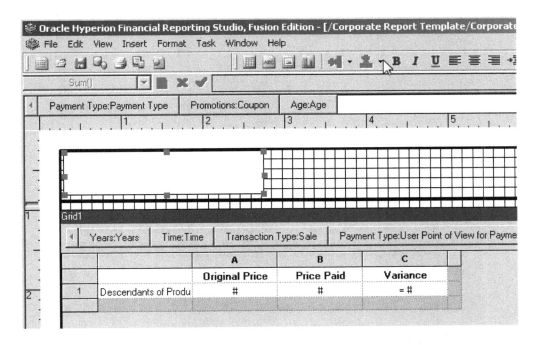

The next step is to populate the text box. In the example, a static report title is added in plain text.

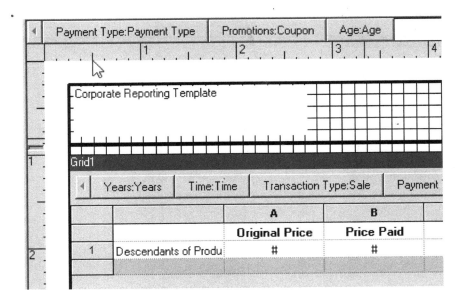

Continuing with the example, the font is formatted. Text fonts are changed by selecting the text in the text object and then selecting the font shortcut on the toolbar, or by selecting the Font item from the Format menu as shown.

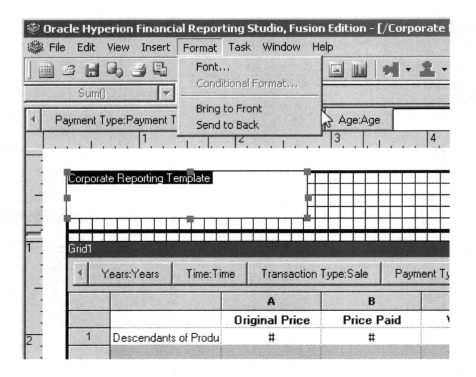

The font may be adjusted to the desired font, size, and appearance through the font window.

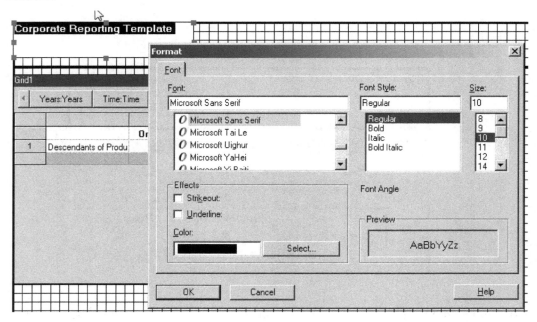

Once the formatting is complete, selecting the OK button applies the changes to the selected text in the text label object.

A single text object may contain text with different font configurations by highlighting the text of interest before modifying the font. This flexibility allows for the population of multiple types of text inside one object.

Displaying the User Point of View Selections in the Header

A major component of many financial reports is the option of creating dynamic reports that allow users to select specific dimension values at runtime. When a user runs a report in PDF format, the user selections are not shown by default on the PDF. Financial Reporting contains functions commonly added to a text label to derive the values selected by the user.

The function **POVAlias** is used for deriving the alias of the member selected in the User Point of View. In the example, the report POV contains three dimensions: Payment Type, Promotions, and Age. The functions are added to a text object simply by typing the function with additional information to alert the text object to the function. The following screenshot shows the three POVAlias functions added to the text object with the appropriate text wrapping.

Take specific notice of the POVAlias function. The function is encased on either side by two sets of carrots: << and >>. An example line of the text object is displayed as follows:

```
Payment Type: <<POVAlias("grid1",Payment Type)>>
```

The POVAlias function takes two arguments to return a value. The first argument is the name of the grid and the second argument is the name of the dimension of interest. Since the function is encased within specific syntax to identify the text as a function, the function may be combined with regular text to better describe the output from the function. In the example above, the dimension name is set in regular text with a colon before the function to describe the output of the function. When the example report is executed, the report displays the dimension name and then the output from the user selection. The following screenshot shows a Point of View with selections made to demonstrate the functionality of the POVAlias function on the example report.

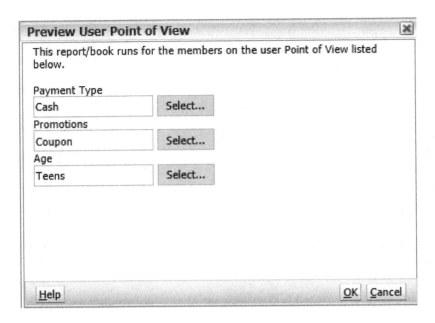

The report output shows the User Point of View selections, made in the screenshot above, dynamically reflected in the report title as shown.

Corporate Reporting Template
Payment Type: Cash
Promotions: Coupon
Age: Teens

	Original Price	Price Paid
Digital Cameras	2,220	1,887
Camcorders	5,018	4,265
Photo Printers	3,916	3,329
Digital Cameras/Camcorders	11,154	9,481

Building the Footer

Footers may contain any content of interest. Many footer sections display information describing the report. Financial Reporting contains many built-in functions for accessing the metadata of a report, providing ways to display descriptive content about the report. After drawing a text object on the report in the footer section, functions are added into the text object by typing the function or through use of the **Insert Function** button located in the Text Properties window, shown in the following screenshot.

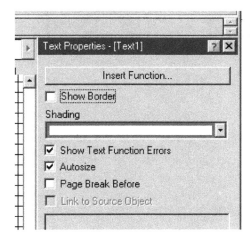

Pressing the Insert Function button opens the Insert Function window with a list of available functions shown on the left of the window.

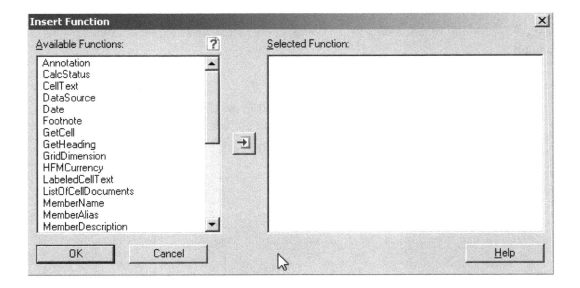

Functions are selected one-by-one and moved into the Selected Function window pane. The Selected Function pane is an editable text area for building out the function or a combination of functions. The following screenshot shows the addition of the ReportName and ReportRunBy functions to the Selected Function pane.

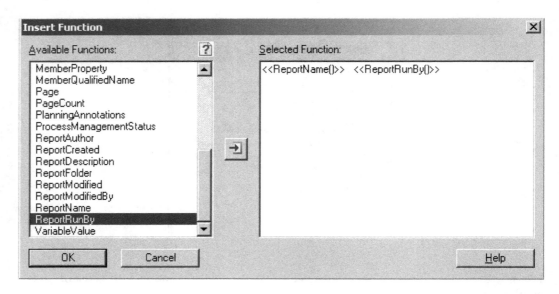

While the functions were selected by the list on the left, the functions could easily be typed into the Selected Function window pane. Notice that the functions in the text box are encased in the function wrapping << and >> characters as seen in the previous example.

> Notice the POVAlias function *is not* contained in the list of functions. There are functions that exist in Financial Reporting that are not part of the Function Selection window. Information on the full list of additional functions is found in the Financial Reporting Studio Users Guide.

Arranging the functions in the desired configuration and pressing OK loads the function text into the text object on the report as shown in the following screenshot.

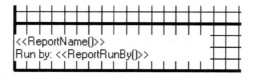

> Moving text in the text object to a separate line (line break) is completed by pressing *Shift + Enter*.

Additional footer items may include company-specific information, page numbers, or additional content and even values from grids in the report. The following screenshot shows the rest of the example report with the footer configured with text objects that display a company's proprietary message as well as the page number and total page count.

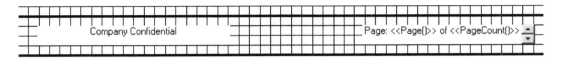

Running the report shows the footer as follows (shrunk for display purposes).

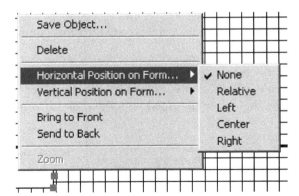

Object Positioning Options

In addition to the standard drag and move functionality in the Studio, a few options exist to control the location of objects on the screen. The **Horizontal Position on Form** and **Vertical Position on Form** buttons can be helpful when positioning objects. The following screenshot shows the right-click menu of the text object. Selecting one of the options from the Horizontal Position on Form menu moves the item across the screen to the appropriate location.

Similarly, selecting one of the options from the Vertical Position on Form menu moves the object across the vertical plane but the object stays constrained within the located section. Therefore, if an object is set to the top of the footer, the object relocates to the top of the footer section while maintaining the same horizontal location.

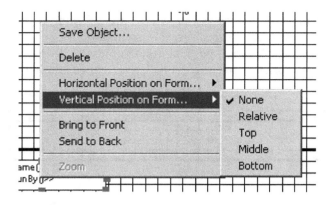

Note: Clicking on the object and moving the object manually, after making a Position on Form change, resets the Position on Form selection to None.

Trouble Moving Objects?

When working with the Financial Reporting Studio software, situations exist when an object may not move from its position. If this occurs, try resizing the object first before moving the object to the desired location. This usually clears up the issue and then the object may be resized back to its original size after the move.

Saving Objects into the Repository

In larger environments, there may be interest in saving objects created on the report into the EPM Workspace repository for use across multiple reports. The *saved objects* may be any object on the report; images and text objects are the most common objects saved and reused.

An object is saved into the repository by selecting the **Save Object** menu item from the right-click menu or from the File menu with the object highlighted. The following screenshot shows the Oracle logo highlighted with the right-click menu open.

Selecting the Save Object menu item opens the Save Object window to the Hyperion Workspace File System as shown in the following screenshot.

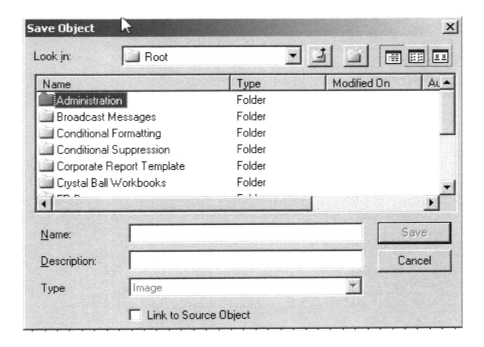

Notice the object type is grayed out and set to the actual object type from the individual report. The saved object can be saved in any folder of the Workspace. After navigating to the folder of interest, a name is added for the object, and the object is saved into the repository by selecting the Save button.

Inserting a Saved Object on a Report

Adding a saved object to a report is completed by selecting the Saved Object menu item from the Insert menu as shown in the following screenshot.

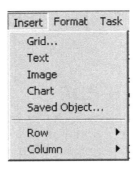

Upon selecting the Saved Object menu item, the Insert Saved Object window appears.

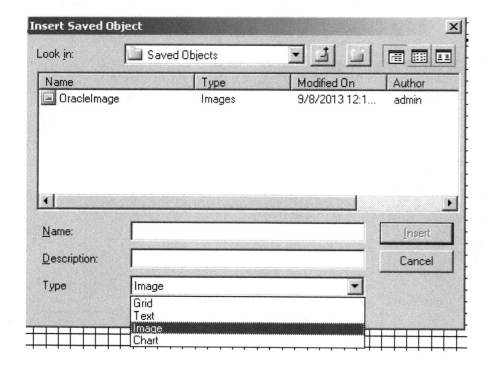

The saved object's type must be selected in the drop-down for the object to appear in the window for selection. Switching the type to image brings up the Oracle image that was saved in the previous example. Selecting image and pressing the Insert button inserts the object into the report.

Managing Saved Objects

The saved object feature allows Financial Reporting developers to template specific objects in a report. Using the template approach allows a single object to be referenced in multiple reports. This feature is incredibly useful for maintaining reports, because a single object is referenced across multiple reports. If the object is changed, the updated object cascades across all of the reports where it is referenced. This feature is also dangerous, because deleting or inappropriately modifying the saved object negatively impacts reports with the referenced object. Use caution and effective planning when using saved objects.

Previewing in HTML & PDF

While working through the report development process, it is important to preview the report to see the rendering in HTML and PDF formats. Both the HTML and PDF formats are previewed from the Financial Reporting interface through the icons on the designer toolbar or by selecting PDF Preview or HTML Preview from the File menu. Upon selecting one of the options, the report is run and renders in either a PDF or HTML page respectively.

> Make sure to test the layout of the reports in *both* HTML and PDF versions throughout the development process to prevent rework. It is recommended to test print the reports to make sure the layout is printing appropriately.

Print Preview and Printing

Since Financial Reporting is commonly used for creating highly formatted, pixel perfect reports, it provides the ability to preview and print reports directly from the Financial Reporting Studio. The report displays exactly the same as printing from the Workspace, and the printout almost always exactly mirrors the on-screen display. While this feature is available, users are also encouraged to preview the reports in PDF and print from the Adobe Acrobat Reader application to ensure accuracy while testing.

Summary

Building a standard reporting template and adding branding to reports improves report aesthetics and brings consistency to organizational reporting. This chapter provided information on building a standard reporting template with derivations of user selections and report metadata in the report output. The chapter started with an overview of the page configuration as it relates to building a standard template. Page size, layout, and margins were discussed for configuring the report display. The chapter continued into the configuration of report headers and footers. Importing images and text objects was demonstrated, and the methods for deriving values from the User Point of View and general report functions were introduced. The chapter then continued with the discussion of object positioning and finally transitioned into saved objects and managing saved objects in an enterprise environment.

10

Financial Reporting Books

A *briefing book* is common to many organizations and combines standard company financial and business information alongside referenced content to produce a repeatable standard deliverable. Oracle provides a feature called a **Financial Reporting Book** which allows for the combination of multiple reports as well as external files into a single package. It provides the ability to execute reports in the book across different business hierarchies with a separate output for each combination. The output can be viewed as a single PDF output or individual files. The books can also be batched (automated), preventing the need to run individual reports or sets of reports to provide the desired output. This chapter demonstrates the functionality of Financial Reporting Books and the benefits realized when using this feature.

The following content is introduced in this chapter:

- Designing a Financial Reporting Book
- Creating a Financial Reporting Book
- Running a Financial Reporting Book
- Supplementing Books with External Files
- Demonstrating the Benefits of Member Selection Functions in Books

Designing a Financial Reporting Book

A Financial Reporting Book is an end-user feature, providing people with the ability to set and configure custom books through the features included in Workspace. Books may contain a single financial report or a set of reports and external files to provide supporting detail. Books allow several reports to be run in a defined sequence, preparing output pages in the order of the selection. Prompts may be managed at the book level or the individual report level, and the book management interface provides easy maintenance.

When designing a book, it is important to identify the reports needed for the book as well as the appearance of the desired output. Considering the *purpose* of the book and its output are keys to the design of the layout. For example, if the purpose of the book is to show summary level information at the front of the book with supporting detail following the summary, the reports should be designed, ordered correctly, and parameters configured to support this approach. In most environments, reports created for individual use will support inclusion in a book, but situations may occur when the prompts and layout of the report may need to be redesigned to support book requirements. Examples include reports with more than one User Point of View.

Users should also be aware that poor performing reports in books compound runtime. Books do not increase the performance of individual reports, and poorly performing reports may strain system resources. Reports and books should be tested for performance after their creation to ensure efficient processing and system resource usage.

Creating a Financial Reporting Book

The first step in creating a Financial Reporting Book is to access the EPM Workspace. Once logged in, a book is created by selecting a New Document through the File menu as shown in the following screenshot.

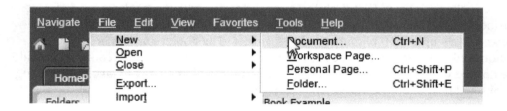

Upon selecting the New Document menu item, a new tab appears with the name New Document 1 and a set of options. Select the Collect Reports into a Book option and then select the Next button as shown in the following screenshot.

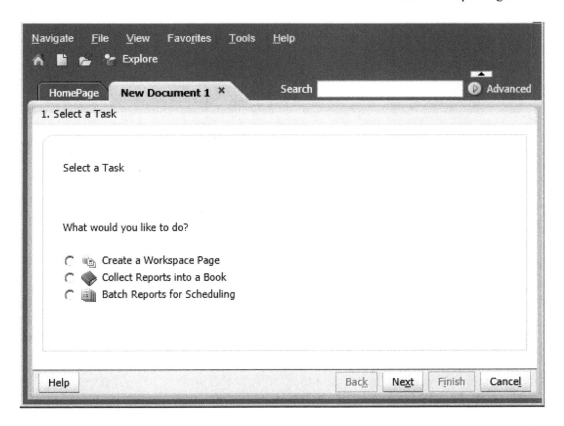

After selecting Collect Reports into a Book, the interface opens to a new window for choosing the reports to run in the book. This chapter uses example reports created earlier in the book to demonstrate book functionality. A report is added to the book by navigating to the folder containing the desired report, selecting it, and clicking the highlighted arrow to move the report into the Selected Items section as shown in the following screenshot.

Chapter 10

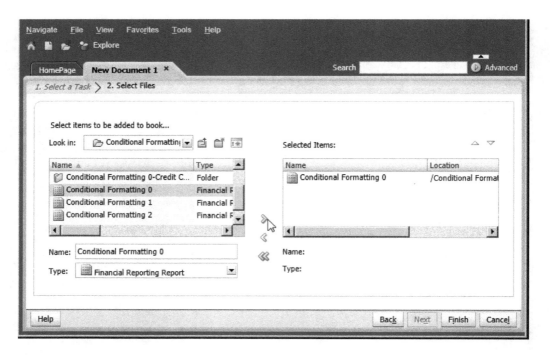

Once the report is selected (in this case the Conditional Formatting 0 report), pressing Finish opens the New Book window as shown in the following screenshot.

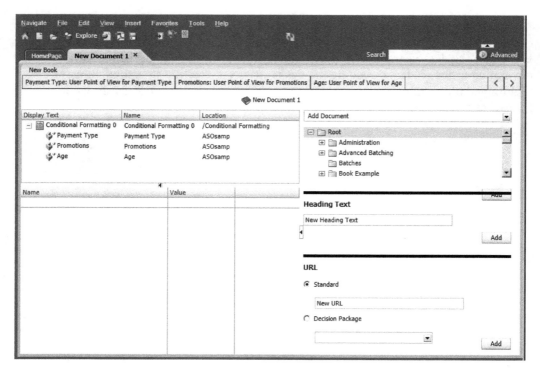

The New Book screen has a set of controls for the report selected, including a new toolbar for facilitating book functions, a section to add additional content, and a section for modifying book settings. The top of the window displays the User Point of View for all reports, in this case Payment Type, Promotions and Age. The window in the top right corner contains a drop-down to add a new document to the book as well as Workspace navigation for selecting additional reports. Additionally, the drop-down can be changed to Book Setup, displaying all of the high-level book configuration items. The following screenshot displays the configuration items available.

Book Setup	▼

General

Name	Value
Paper Size:	Lette ▼
Consecutive Page Numbers	Yes ▼
Include Table of Contents in Page Numbering	No ▼
Collate Reports By:	Repo ▼
Include Related Content in Batch Output	No ▼
Starting Page Number:	1
Enable Embedded Content Processing	No ▼

Table of Contents

Name	Value
Include in Printed Output	Yes ▼
Orientation	Portr ▼
ASOsamp	Mem ▼

The setup screen is fairly straightforward with various configuration options available for the report's display and table of contents. Notice the database connection name at the bottom of the table of contents. The member name or an alias, for each database connection, can be selected for every member in the table of contents.

The left side of the interface has two sections, shown in the following screenshot. The top shows the reports added to the book and the User Point of View for each report, and the bottom section provides a set of options for each item selected in the top menu.

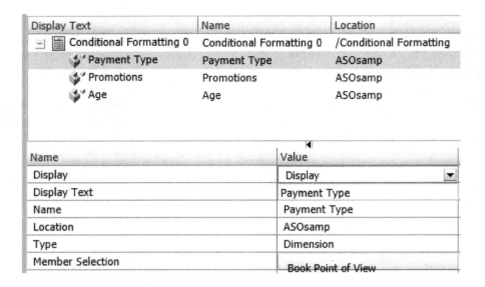

Notice the bottom section offers a way to display or hide the member and a means to select the members for each report. This feature is key to the book and drives its output. In this example, the book displays the breakout of all Payment Types with the ability to select a Promotions and Age member from the User Point of View.

Double-clicking on Payment Type in the top window or selecting the **Book Point of View** button on the bottom section opens the Preview User Point of View window shown below.

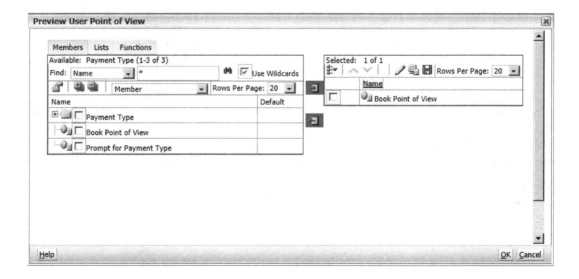

The current setting for the Point of View is the Book Point of View. The book Point of View setting denotes that the Payment Type dimension receives its value from the Point of View for the overall book. This setting is a template setting, allowing a single Point of View to control multiple reports.

Moving the example forwards, the Book Point of View is removed from the selection and Children (of Payment Type) is selected by navigating to the Functions menu, selecting the checkbox for Children then moving the item to the selected area as shown in the following screenshot.

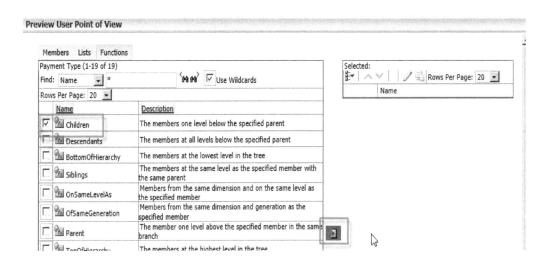

When the function is moved to the selected area, a window appears for configuring the function options. In this case, Member is selected by pressing the magnifying glass icon and selecting Payment Type from the member selection window.

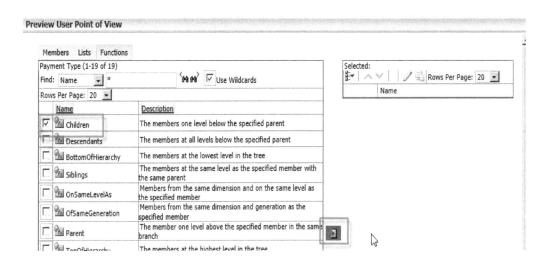

After pressing OK, Children of Payment Type now displays in the book preview window as shown.

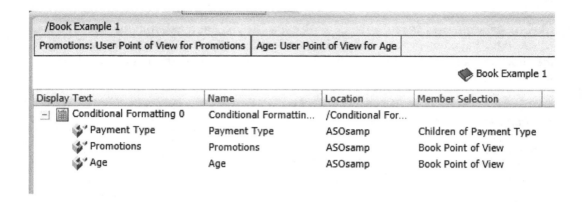

Note: In books with more than one report, the Point of View selections made in one report can be individually copied by right-clicking on the User Point of View in the selection screen, selecting Copy Member Selection To, and selecting the target report.

Also, notice at the top of the window how the Point of View for the book now only contains the two members set to Book Point of View. At this time, the book is saved by using the File menu with the name Book Example 1. The saved book now appears in Workspace with the name and the book icon, as shown below.

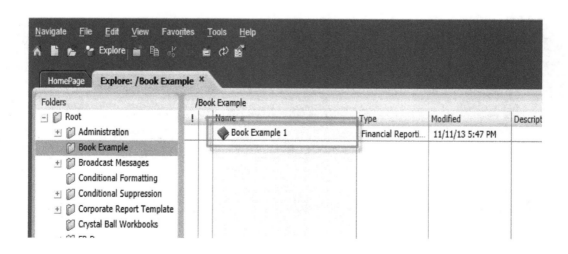

Running a Financial Reporting Book

When a book is ready for execution, there are three options available: HTML Preview, PDF Preview, and Complete Book in PDF. Running a book is similar to running a standard report. When the book is run, the User Point of View displays (if one exists for the book) as shown in the following screenshot.

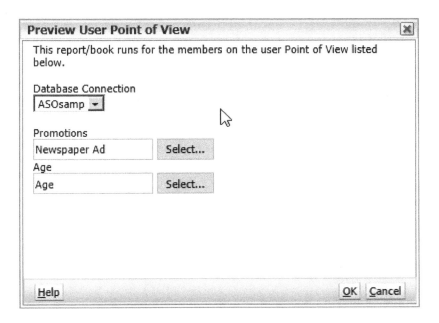

Note: If a book utilizes reports that have different database connections, there is a dropdown which allows a user to switch to that database connection and set any POVs that might need to be defined.

In this example, the book was run in HTML Preview mode. The Promotions item is set to Newspaper Ad and Age is left at the top of the dimension. After making the selection, the book is run and a new tab appears with the book output listed.

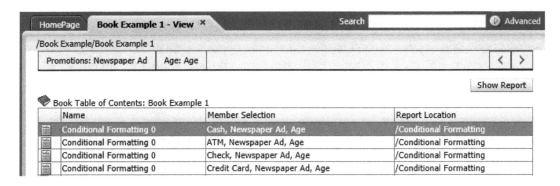

The book ran the Conditional Formatting 0 report for each *child* of the Payment Type dimension. Each output displays the report name, member selection, and the report location. The output is displayed by selecting the report and pressing the Show Report button (top-right of the screen). Selecting the first output and pressing the Show Report button opens the output in a new tab as shown below.

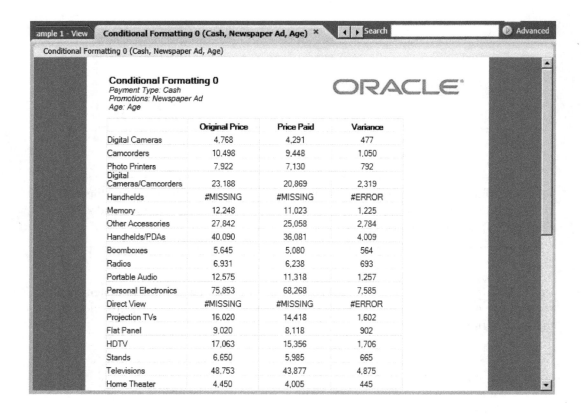

Similarly, the book can be executed in PDF Preview mode, with the output displayed as a PDF instead of an HTML file.

While the preview mode is commonly utilized to obtain selected output from the book, books are most commonly run as a complete PDF with a table of contents. Selecting the Complete Book in PDF menu item when running the book executes all of the files in the book and catalogues them with a table of contents (if enabled) in a new tab. The following screenshot shows the book executed completely in PDF format.

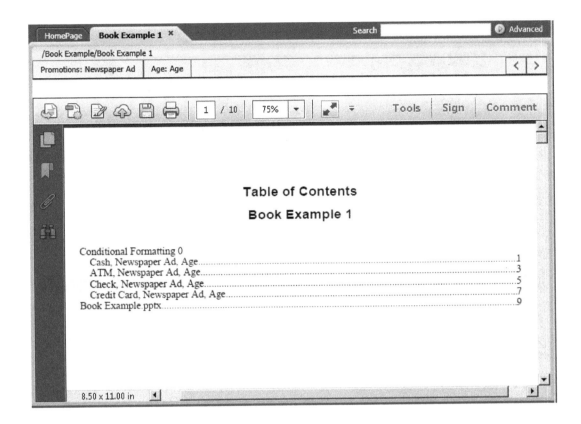

The table of contents is the first page of the document and each report is displayed thereafter in hierarchy member order. Each link in the table of contents is navigable. Additionally, a PowerPoint file was also added to the book, which is discussed below.

A Note on Batching

Financial Reporting Books can also be added to a batch process. Batching allows the Oracle EPM Scheduler to execute the book at a desired time using standard POV values or a list of inputs to populate a POV for the purpose of creating individual data snapshots for each book. This feature is very powerful, allowing for the automated batch creation of briefing books without the need to run the book multiple times with different POV values. Book batching is described in the next chapter, *Financial Reporting Batches*.

Supplementing Books with External Files

Books now support the inclusion of external files including MS office, PDF, and other specific file types. When including external content, the file of interest needs to be imported into Workspace. This import is completed by importing a file through the File → Import → File menu item as shown in the following screenshot.

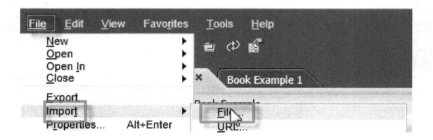

Browsing the local machine for the file of interest and then selecting Finish adds the file to Workspace for inclusion in the book.

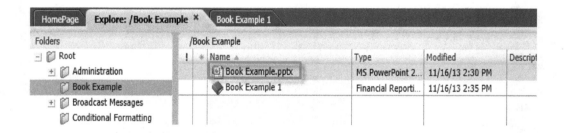

With the file now in Workspace, the file can be added to the book. A book is edited by selecting the book and opening it in the Editor mode. The external file is added by navigating to the file in the Add Document section, selecting the file, and then pressing the Add button.

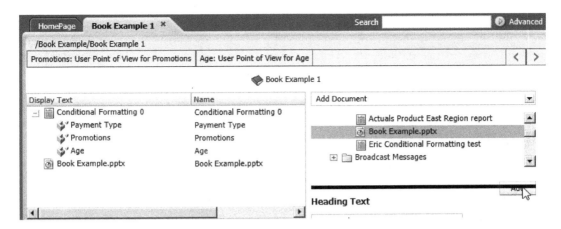

Once completed, the file moves over to the left pane of the screen (also demonstrated in the screenshot above). Once the file is added to the book, properties can be added by selecting the file and customizing the bottom pane as shown below.

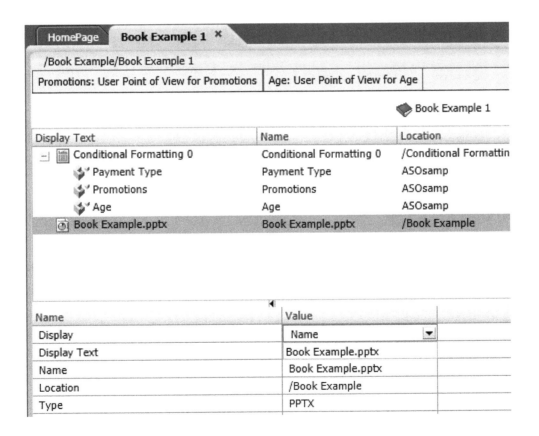

The name of the file can be omitted or displayed along with custom text and the file description. Selecting the custom text option for the display allows the name to be edited in the display text field. Once the configuration is complete, the file displays inside the book at the location provided.

Demonstrating the Benefits of Member Selection Functions in Books

The book created in the example above was very simple and used only the Children function for one of the Point of Views. Functions are very powerful and allow for greater customization of a book's output.

Descendants

The **Descendants** function displays the members at all levels below the selected member. Below, the Age dimension is edited to show all descendants of the entire hierarchy.

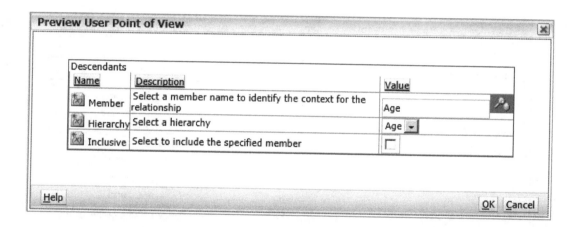

When run, the report displays output for both Payment Type and Age as shown below.

```
Conditional Formatting 0
   Cash, Newspaper Ad, Teens............................................................1
   Cash, Newspaper Ad, 1 to 13 Years..................................................3
   Cash, Newspaper Ad, 14 to 19 Years................................................5
   Cash, Newspaper Ad, Adults...........................................................7
   Cash, Newspaper Ad, 20 to 25 Years................................................9
   Cash, Newspaper Ad, 26 to 30 Years..............................................11
   Cash, Newspaper Ad, 31 to 35 Years..............................................13
   Cash, Newspaper Ad, 36 to 45 Years..............................................15
   Cash, Newspaper Ad, 46 to 54 Years..............................................17
   Cash, Newspaper Ad, Senior..........................................................19
   Cash, Newspaper Ad, 55 to 64 Years..............................................21
```

Since Age is the top member of the dimension, all members below Age are displayed for each of the Payment Types.

Notice that the member Age is not displayed in the output. The Inclusive checkbox can be added to any of the hierarchical functions to display the selected member as well.

BottomOfHierarchy

The **BottomOfHierarchy** function pulls all Level 0 members in the specified dimension. No additional criteria are applied to this function and the entire set of Level 0 members are returned. When executed, the example book displays all Level 0 members of the Age dimension for each Payment Type.

```
Conditional Formatting 0
   Cash, Newspaper Ad, 1 to 13 Years..................................................1
   Cash, Newspaper Ad, 14 to 19 Years................................................3
   Cash, Newspaper Ad, 20 to 25 Years................................................5
   Cash, Newspaper Ad, 26 to 30 Years................................................7
   Cash, Newspaper Ad, 31 to 35 Years................................................9
   Cash, Newspaper Ad, 36 to 45 Years..............................................11
   Cash, Newspaper Ad, 46 to 54 Years..............................................13
   Cash, Newspaper Ad, 55 to 64 Years..............................................15
   Cash, Newspaper Ad, 65+ years.....................................................17
   ATM, Newspaper Ad, 1 to 13 Years.................................................19
   ATM, Newspaper Ad, 14 to 19 Years...............................................21
   ATM, Newspaper Ad, 20 to 25 Years...............................................23
   ATM, Newspaper Ad, 26 to 30 Years...............................................25
   ATM, Newspaper Ad, 31 to 35 Years...............................................27
   ATM, Newspaper Ad, 36 to 45 Years...............................................29
```

Siblings

The **Siblings** function pulls all members with the same parent as the selected member. Setting this function on the Age dimension with the selection Teens displays as follows, and includes Adults and Seniors which are the only two other siblings of Teens in the hierarchy.

```
Conditional Formatting 0
    Cash, Newspaper Ad, Adults..................................................................................1
    Cash, Newspaper Ad, Senior..................................................................................3
    ATM, Newspaper Ad, Adults...................................................................................5
    ATM, Newspaper Ad, Senior...................................................................................7
    Check, Newspaper Ad, Adults.................................................................................9
    Check, Newspaper Ad, Senior.................................................................................11
    Credit Card, Newspaper Ad, Adults..........................................................................13
    Credit Card, Newspaper Ad, Senior..........................................................................15
```

Note the Teens member was not included. Similar to the Descendants function, setting the Inclusive checkbox includes the Teens member in the output.

OnSameLevelAs

The **OnSameLevelAs** function pulls all members from the same level as the selected member. This function is similar to the siblings function, but the function expands the selection to all members at the same level in the hierarchy (not just the local section). In the example, the 1 to 13 Years member is selected in the function displaying all of the year range members across all Payment Types.

```
Conditional Formatting 0
    Cash, Newspaper Ad, 1 to 13 Years..........................................................................1
    Cash, Newspaper Ad, 14 to 19 Years.........................................................................3
    Cash, Newspaper Ad, 20 to 25 Years.........................................................................5
    Cash, Newspaper Ad, 26 to 30 Years.........................................................................7
    Cash, Newspaper Ad, 31 to 35 Years.........................................................................9
    Cash, Newspaper Ad, 36 to 45 Years.........................................................................11
    Cash, Newspaper Ad, 46 to 54 Years.........................................................................13
    Cash, Newspaper Ad, 55 to 64 Years.........................................................................15
```

Parent

The **Parent** function pulls the parent member of the selection. This function is commonly used with a Book Point of View selection to display the parent member of a selection. In this example the member 1 to 13 Years was selected as the member while the Parent of the selected member is the Teens member. The following output is displayed when the book is executed.

Ancestors

The **Ancestors** function pulls all members *above* the specified member in the hierarchy. In this example, the 1 to 13 Years member is selected which displays the parent Teens and Age members of the hierarchy.

```
Conditional Formatting 0
    Cash, Newspaper Ad, Age.................................................................1
    Cash, Newspaper Ad, Teens..............................................................3
    ATM, Newspaper Ad, Age................................................................5
    ATM, Newspaper Ad, Teens.............................................................7
    Check, Newspaper Ad, Age..............................................................9
    Check, Newspaper Ad, Teens..........................................................11
    Credit Card, Newspaper Ad, Age.....................................................13
    Credit Card, Newspaper Ad, Teens..................................................15
```

Range

The **Range** function allows for members inside a specified start and end member to be selected. In this example, the StartMember is set to 1 to 13 Years and the EndMember is 31 to 35 Years. The configuration of the function window is displayed as follows.

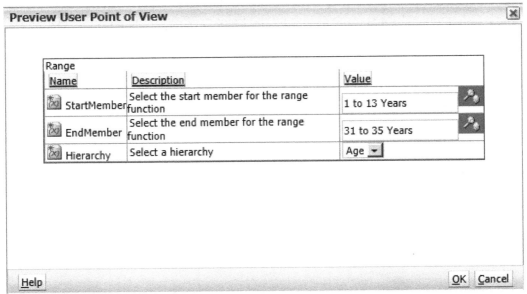

Executing the report shows the Age range specified for all Payment Types.

Summary

Books enhance the capabilities of Financial Reporting by providing a powerful end-user feature used to compile a set of reports into a single deliverable with automated execution. Books effectively combine multiple reports, execute reports multiple times using dynamic hierarchical content, and create a common view of information for use across an organization. Books take advantage of reports that contain user Points of View, which provide the ability to specify reporting parameters in the book configuration. This parameterization allows a wide-range of reports to be executed using the same parameters for each selectable dimension across all reports in the book.

This chapter started with the creation of a book and addressed all of the initial configuration settings and book level parameters. The chapter described the steps to add reports to a book and the steps to configure the Point of View at the report level and at the overall book level. The chapter described the recent feature for adding external files to enhance book features, and the chapter demonstrated methods of using functions in member selection to make books dynamic. The chapter touched on the ability to run a book using the scheduling utility with the use of a parametrization file, which is discussed in the next chapter, *Financial Reporting Batches*.

11

Financial Reporting Batches

A **Financial Reporting Batch** is a way to automatically execute a Financial Reporting report or book for a particular date/time and set of input parameters. Batches are created in Workspace and utilize the **Scheduler** to run and manage the batch job. The Scheduler provides the ability to run the job immediately or schedule it for a particular date or time. The Scheduler manages the output, which can be saved in folders in the Workspace, emailed, or even sent to a local network shared drive.

Batches are most commonly used to execute the same object for multiple point of view selections with a disbursement to a wide user community. This feature allows the batch scheduler to manage the time the report is run, the input parameters, and the output methods *without* requiring a user to manually run and distribute each report.

The following topics are introduced in this chapter:

- Creating Financial Reporting Batches
- Scheduling Batches
- Job Status, Monitoring, and Modifications
- Batching Financial Reporting Books
- Batch Bursting using a Burst File

Creating a Financial Reporting Batch

Batch creation is completed using a few simple steps from Workspace. A new batch is created by selecting the File menu and selecting New → Document as shown in the following screenshot.

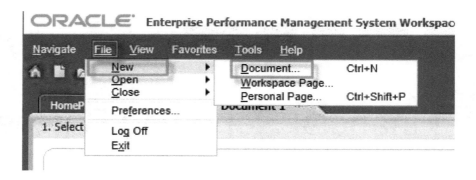

A new tab appears with the name New Document 1 and a set of options, similar to creating a Book. Batch creation is started by selecting the Batch Reports for Scheduling option and then selecting the Next button as shown in the following screenshot.

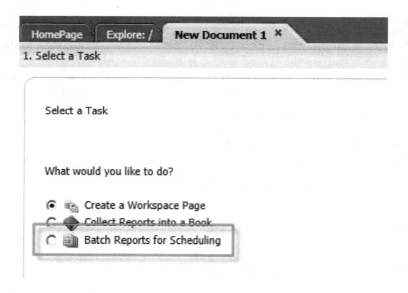

After selecting the batch scheduling option, the interface opens to a new window where the reporting objects are selected.

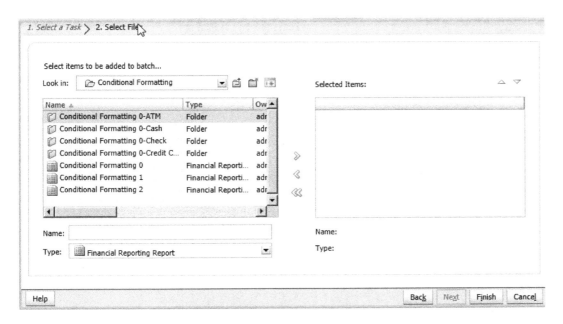

In this example, one of the conditional formatting reports developed earlier in the book is selected. Selecting the report and pressing the right-arrow in the middle pane of the interface moves the selected object into the Selected Items window as shown in the following screenshot.

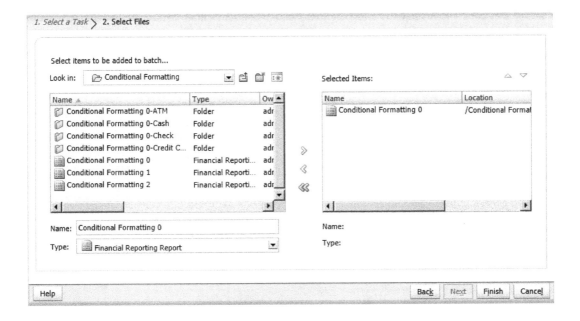

Pressing the Finish button opens a new screen for the batch with the name New Document 1 as shown below.

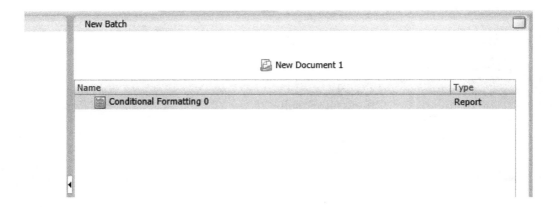

At this point in the process, the file is not saved. Saving the batch is completed by selecting the File menu and selecting Save As. Upon selecting the save option, the following window appears with the ability to save the document into a Workspace folder location with the Financial Reporting Batch file type.

It is strongly recommended to save batch files in a Workspace location dedicated to batching. Batch files are not commonly executed by the general user community, and the files created for batches may clutter general reporting folders.

For this example, a folder called Batches was created and used to store the created batch files.

It is strongly recommended that a name be used for the batch file that indicates the purpose or output of the batch. The Description field may also be utilized to save information about the batch file and output. In this example, the batch file is saved with the name Conditional Formatting report batch. After entering the name, selecting the Save button at the bottom of the window saves the file into the folder and the name of the batch is updated in the interface as shown below.

At this point, the batch is now ready for scheduling.

Scheduling a Financial Reporting Batch

With a batch file created, the next step in the process is to schedule the batch with the Workspace scheduling utility. The **Scheduler** not only schedules the batch file, but provides a set of features for the configuration of the batch output and recipients. Scheduling a batch is completed by selecting the **Batch Scheduler** from the Workspace Navigate → Schedule menu section as shown in the following screenshot.

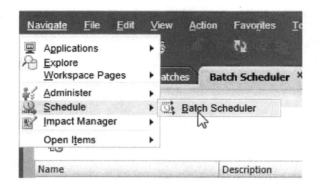

Batch Scheduler

The Batch Scheduler is the interface and engine for managing and executing batch jobs across the entire EPM system. The following is a screenshot of the scheduler interface with two Scheduled Batch jobs populated.

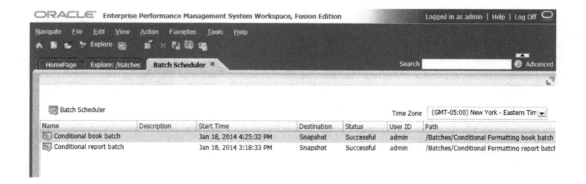

Each batch job contains a set of options including the schedule, user, destination, status, and other configurable information.

Creating a New Scheduled Batch

The first step in running a batch job is to create a new scheduled batch by selecting File → New Scheduled Batch from the Workspace File menu or by right-clicking and selecting New Scheduled Batch from the right-click menu as shown in the following screenshot.

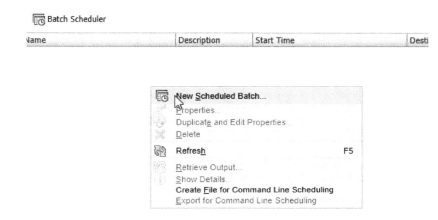

The Scheduled Batch window opens for the configuration of the Batch Job Name and Description.

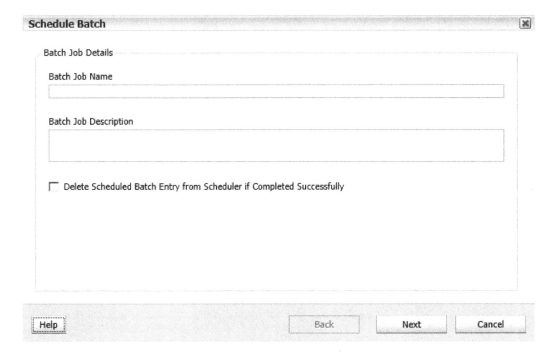

The scheduled batch name and description are displayed in the batch scheduler utility. In this example, the name Conditional Report Batch is used. The third setting in the configuration window is a checkbox for removing the scheduled batch from the scheduler if the job completes successfully at runtime. The **delete entry** feature is commonly used for batch testing or with single-run jobs to prevent the need for extra maintenance or cleaning up the scheduling interface.

After configuring the initial settings, pressing the Next button opens the Schedule Batch window to select the batch file for scheduling.

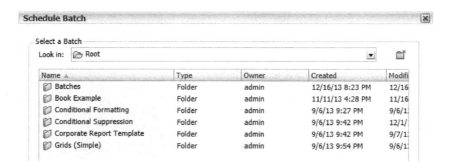

In this example, the batch file is located in the Batches folder of Workspace as shown in the following screenshot.

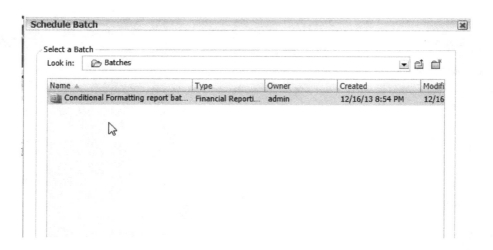

Note: Only *one* batch file may be selected per scheduled job.

Once selected, pressing the Next button opens the batch configuration settings screen.

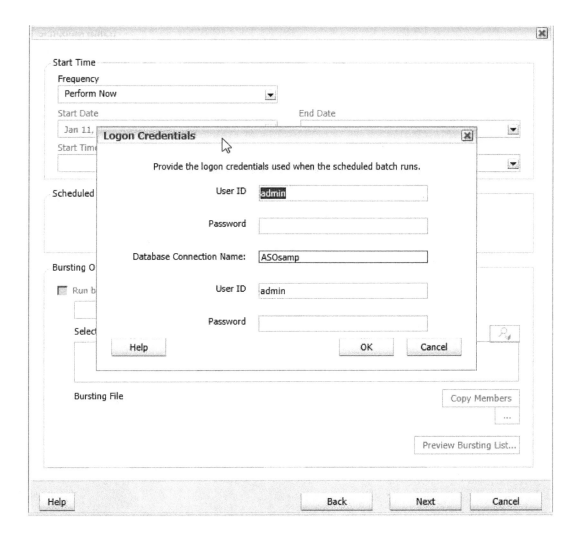

The configuration window appears with the Login Configuration pop-up window for entering Financial Reporting credentials as well as the credentials for the database connections.

Hyperion implementations across businesses impart varying controls on users building and executing batches. Some environments allow users to schedule batches and others make batch scheduling an administrative feature. The Oracle EPM system is configured to support either approach, with Shared Services controlling access to the Job Scheduling roles for each user/group.

In this example, the administrator account is utilized for both logins. After entering the appropriate credentials and selecting the OK button, the Logon Credentials window closes and the Schedule Batch window appears with the first set of configurable options.

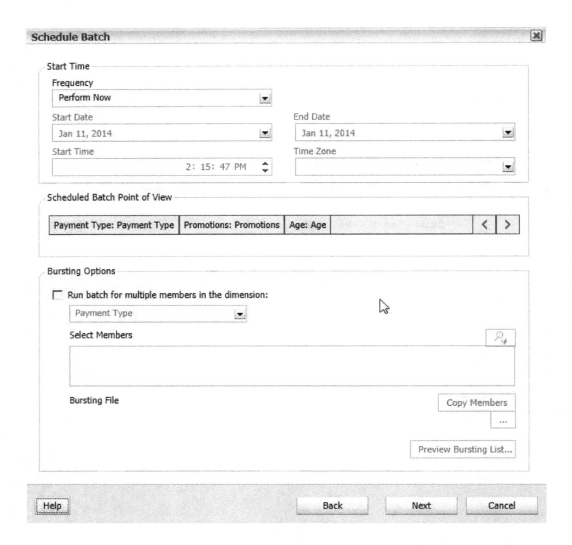

Setting the Batch Frequency

The first step in setting the schedule is selecting the runtime and frequency. The top of the schedule window contains a **Start Time** section for setting the execution time of the report. The section contains a Frequency drop-down as well as Start Date, End Date, Start Time and Time Zone settings.

Notice the frequency default is set to Perform Now, with all of the other time options disabled. The Perform Now setting executes the batch as soon as the configuration interface is complete. Batch jobs may also be scheduled to run based on different frequencies. The following screenshot shows the list of frequency options.

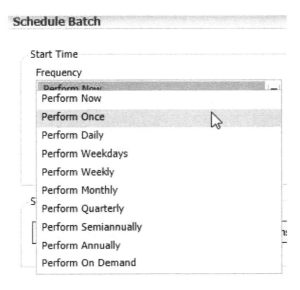

This example uses the Perform Once setting to demonstrate available runtime features. The following screenshot displays the available options after Perform Once is selected.

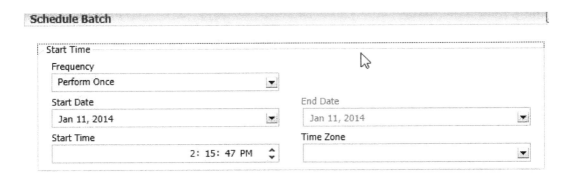

All of the options except for the End Date setting are enabled for selection. Selecting the Start Date drop-down displays a calendar, allowing a user to run the batch on a specific date. Notice the calendar opens to the current month and arrows exist to navigate to future months and years.

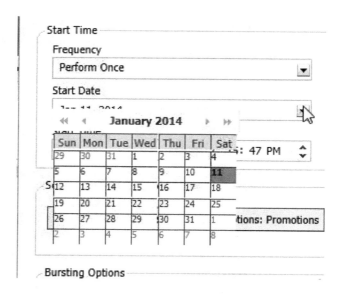

After selecting the date of interest, it is populated in the Start Date window.

For comparison purposes, selecting Perform Daily allows for the configuration of the End Date as shown in the following screenshot. The scheduled job in this case executes daily at the specified Start Time on each day starting with the Start Date with the last day being the End Date.

Returning to the Perform Once option, setting the Start Time is required to finalize the job schedule with Time Zone as an optional setting.

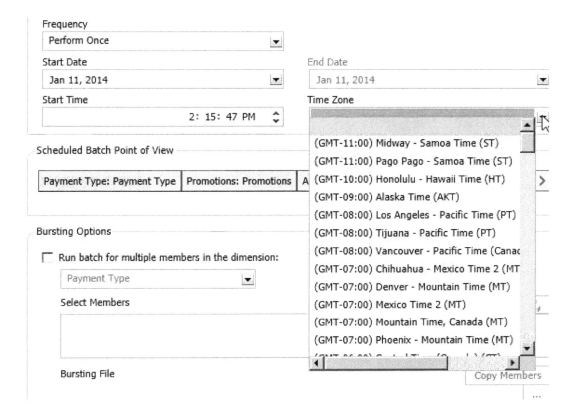

The Start Time is entered by using the up and down arrows or by manually entering the time into the box. The Time Zone drop-down allows a user to specify the Time Zone when the batch is run. The Time Zone setting is especially useful when dealing with job outputs for global offices/locations.

> Note: The run schedule may be modified at any time by modifying the scheduled batch job.

Scheduled Batch Point of View

The **Scheduled Batch Point of View** is under the Start Time section and is used to set Point of View values for batch reports. The screenshot below shows the Scheduled Batch Point of View configuration utility.

Clicking on a specific dimension in the Point of View line displays the Preview User Point of View window as shown in the following screenshot.

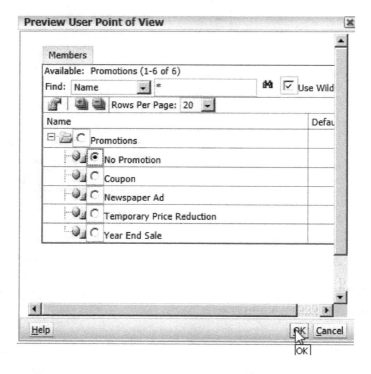

Notice that only *one* member may be selected for each Point of View in the Scheduled Batch Point of View, with only one dimension allowed for multiple outputs through **Bursting**. In this example, the No Promotion option is selected for the Promotions Point of View, the Age Point of View remains at the top of the dimension, and the Payment Type is set to the Bursting option.

Batch Bursting with Manual Selection

Bursting is a powerful optional setting used to create separate outputs for a list of inputs for only one Point of View in a batch. When the scheduled batch is executed, the batch is executed in a loop for each input in the bursting configuration. The implications of the one dimension burst limitation have an impact on the number of batches required. If a batch needs to run for multiple members of more than one Point of View, then additional scheduled batch jobs are required.

The following screenshot displays the bursting options for the scheduled batch.

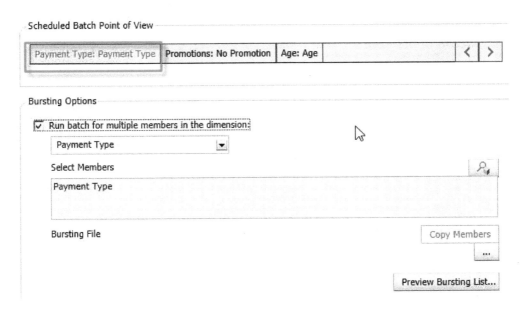

Clicking the checkbox for Run batch for multiple members in the dimension turns on the bursting option. In this example, the Payment Type dimension is set for bursting. When the bursting options are on, the Schedule Batch Point of View section removes the ability to edit the Point of View selection for the dimension selected for bursting.

Setting bursting values is completed by either the manual selection of members or by configuring a burst file. The manual selection of members requires the magnifying glass icon to be pressed and then the members chosen. Upon selecting the magnifying glass, the Preview User Point of View selection window appears as shown.

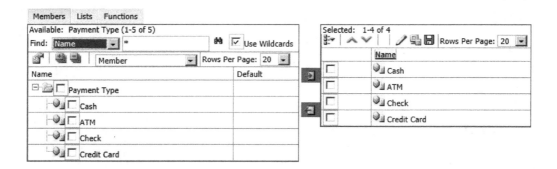

Notice this Point of View selection window contains the means to select multiple members as well as the ability to select lists and functions. In this example, all of the children of the Payment Type member are selected. Selecting the OK button at the bottom of the window populates the Selected Members text box as shown in the following screenshot.

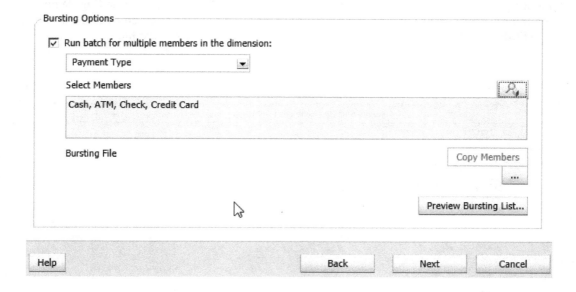

Selecting Next at the bottom of the screen continues the Schedule Batch process to the output configuration screen for selecting the job output. This example continues with the manual selection of bursting options. The final section of this chapter demonstrates configuration and batch execution using a burst file.

Configuring Job Output

The job output screen offers a number of options including storing the job output in Workspace, emailing the output to a list of recipients, and sending the files to a network location.

Saving Job Output to Workspace

The first section in the job output window is **Destinations**, which controls the type and location of the file output. The first option is the Save As Snapshot in Repository feature.

This option saves the batch output, or **Snapshot**, into a folder in Workspace. There are two options for the location of the files. The first option is the In Same Folder as Original Object and batch results are saved where the original batch file is located. The In Another Folder option is used to select another location in Workspace.

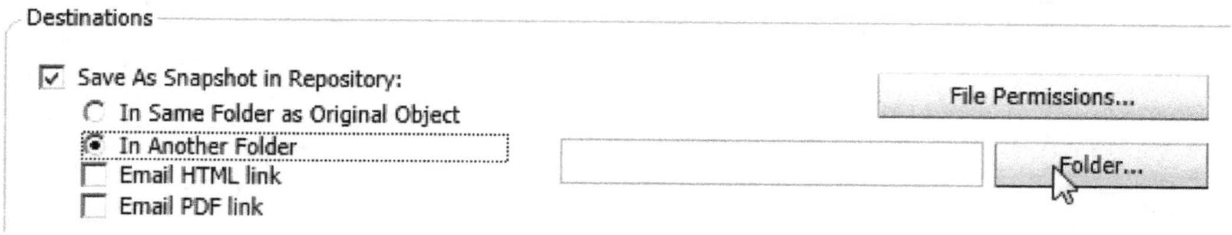

The In Another Folder option is especially helpful for placing output in folders that are accessible by users.

Note: This setting only allows for the selection of one folder. The advanced batch operation example later in the chapter (using a burst file) addresses a newer feature for saving batch outputs into multiple folders.

In this example, the Conditional Reporting folder in Workspace is used for batch output. After choosing the folder of interest, selecting OK adds the folder to the location box as shown in the following screenshot.

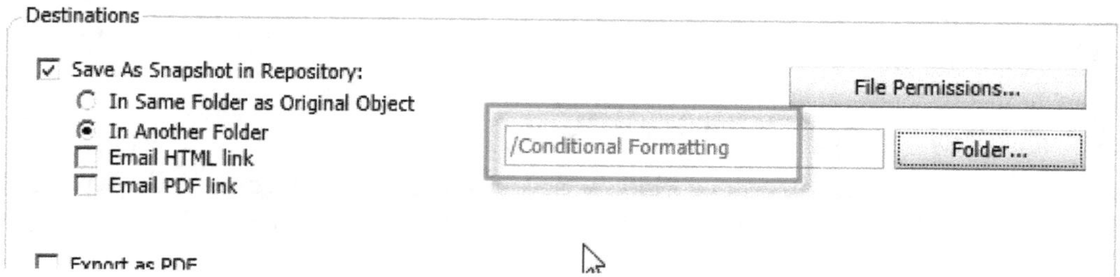

The File Permissions button is used to set the permissions to the job output. When the job output is run, the output is created in HTML and PDF formats. The final two options in this section are to send email links to the HTML/PDF outputs.

Note: The user must have permissions to the folder and snapshot files in Workspace to view the batch content.

Exporting Job Output to a PDF

The second option is **Export as PDF** which offers the means to directly export to PDF files. The following screenshot shows the options for exporting to PDF.

Export as PDF allows for the export of PDF documents to be stored with the job output, sent in an email, or sent to an external directory in the environment. Using an external directory requires a configuration step by system administrators for it to appear in the drop-down. The Email as PDF Attachments option is commonly utilized to send a job in email across an enterprise, but the maintenance of email bursting settings can be time-consuming and tedious. If emailing files, Zip PDF's allows for the zipping of the files to reduce their file size. The last option for Print Annotations is used to include any Financial Reporting annotations set on the report.

Exporting Job Output as HMTL and MHMTL

The scheduler also provides a way to export to HTML and MHTML with the job output or in an external directory. The following screenshot displays the options for exporting to HTML and MHTML.

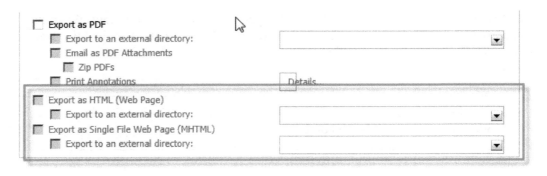

Note: HTML and MHTML export options are not accessible when the bursting option is utilized.

Bursting Output Labels

The final part to the job output screen is the Bursted Output Labels section used to configure file names for each burst files output. The following screenshot shows the default configuration for bursting file names.

A number of functions exist for configuring the output file name. A list of the functions is found by pressing the →Fx button.

Text can also be added, as desired, to each label. Once the expression is configured, pressing the check icon button validates the expression for accuracy.

Configuring PDF Email Output

If the Email as PDF Attachments option is selected in the previous screen, a window appears for the configuration of the email and its recipients. The screenshot below displays the Schedule Batch PDF Email Output window.

207

The interface provides the ability to select recipients and configure a subject and body text for the email. Financial Reporting functions may also be used in the subject and message body to include the report's name, run date/time, and other desired functions.

Configuring Success or Failed Email Output

The final screen for scheduling batches is for configuring emails sent out after the job has executed.

On this screen, the user scheduling the batch can specify whether *successful completion* or *failure* emails are sent out. The checkboxes are used to turn on each job notification email. The following screenshot shows both the successful and failed job notifications configured.

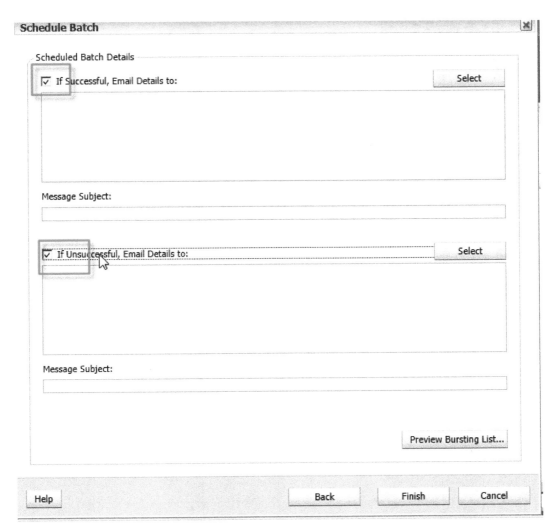

Custom Message Subjects can be setup for successful and failed jobs. Email addresses are added by pressing the Select button in each section and adding email addresses.

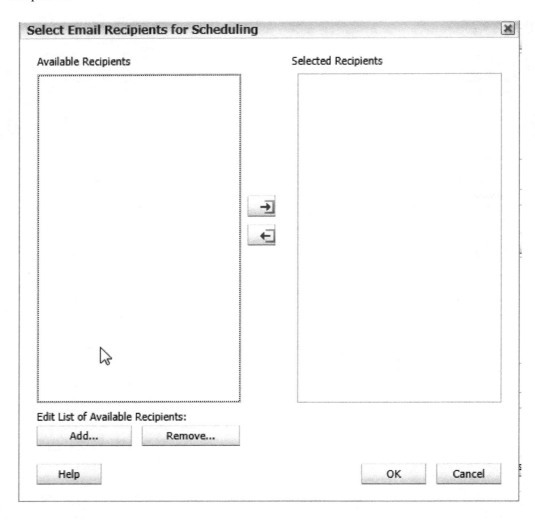

Pressing the Add button at the bottom of the screen brings up the following window for adding email addresses to the list.

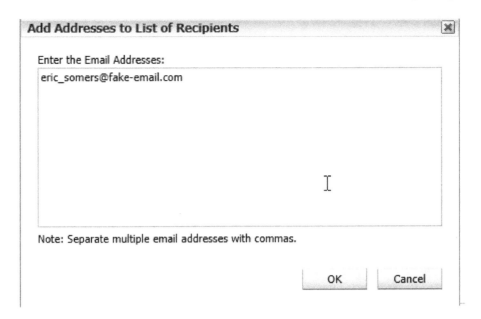

Email addresses can be pasted or typed in, and commas must separate each address. Pressing the OK button adds the emails to the list of Available Recipients. Selecting each address and selecting the arrow button, shown below, sets the email of a selected recipient.

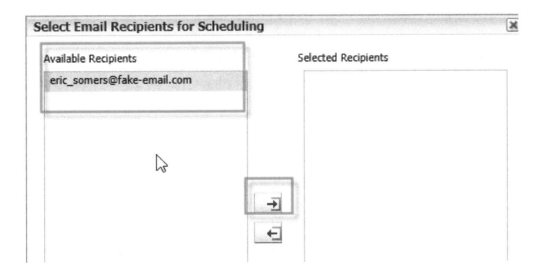

Pressing the OK button at the bottom of the window imports selected email addresses as shown next.

Schedule Batch

Scheduled Batch Details

☑ If Successful, Email Details to: Select

eric_somers@fake-email.com

Message Subject:

Once the email addresses and subjects are configured, pressing the Finish button at the bottom of the window completes the batch configuration and submits the batch to the server for execution. Depending on the scheduling options chosen, the batch may run immediately or at the specified date/time configured.

> Note on Performance: Batches are dependent on the objects used to build the batch. If a report runs for an excessive length of time for one POV selection, the batch will run for a similar length of time for each POV in the burst selection.

Job Status, Monitoring, and Modification Options

After a job is submitted for execution, the main scheduler window conveys the status of the job. The screenshot below shows the job scheduler with a batch running.

Name	Description	Start Time	Destination	Status
Conditional report batch		Jan 18, 2014 3:18:33 PM EST	Snapshot	Running

In the example, the batch completes after a few seconds. Pressing the refresh button in the scheduler toolbar shows the change in status from Running to Successful.

Scheduled Batch Log Information

When a scheduled job completes successfully or fails, a job log is generated. Viewing the log is completed by clicking on the batch and selecting the Action menu and Show Details, or by highlighting the Scheduled Batch, right-clicking, and selecting Show Details from the right-click menu.

The job log file is displayed in a new window; example shown below.

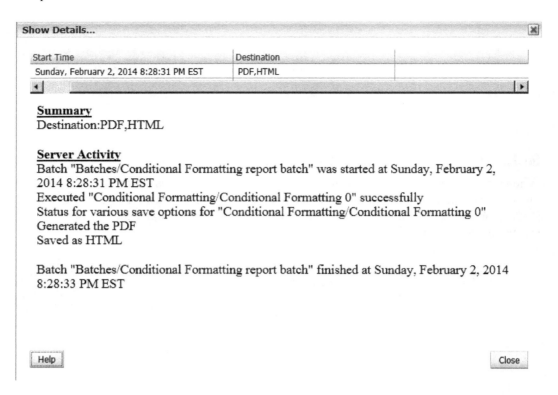

Viewing Snapshot Output

One of the most commonly used features of batching is the **Snapshot** output feature, which saves a **Financial Reporting Snapshot Report** in Workspace in a desired folder with desired permissions. In the example used previously, the batch output was saved in the Conditional Formatting folder in Workspace. Opening the Conditional Formatting folder shows a series of folders, one for each burst of the batch that was executed with the bursting member name in the folder name.

Each folder contains the snapshot report for each specific burst.

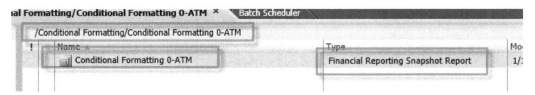

The snapshot saves the data from the report in both HTML and PDF formats. Opening the snapshot in HTML format displays the following content.

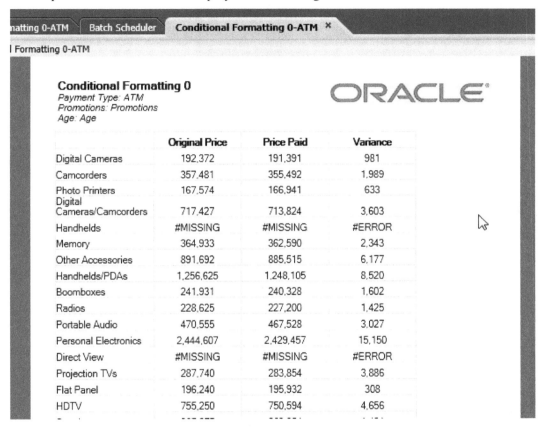

The HTML view and PDF view from the snapshot display in exactly the same way as running the job directly from the Studio or Workspace.

Financial Reporting Output Stored with the Batch

In addition to the snapshot, email, and directory locations, the batch output is stored directly with the batch (unless bursting is utilized). Exports stored with the batch include PDF, HTML, and MHTML formats. Viewing the output is completed by selecting the completed batch in the scheduler, and then selecting Retrieve Output from the Action or right-click menu. When selected, the Retrieve Output window opens and the browser prompts the user for action on the output zip file.

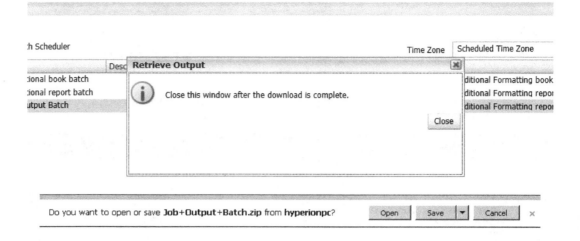

Opening the zip file displays the selected output for the batch (in this case a PDF and an HTML file).

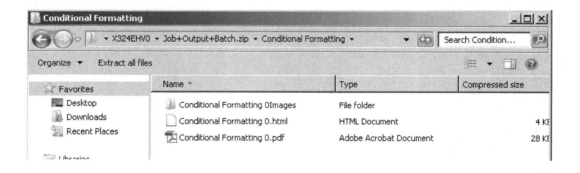

Batching Financial Reporting Books

In addition to batching Financial Reports, **Books** may also be batched, thus providing the ability to batch and burst book contents. A batch file is created with a book by switching the file type to Financial Reporting Book when creating a batch or adding reports to the batch.

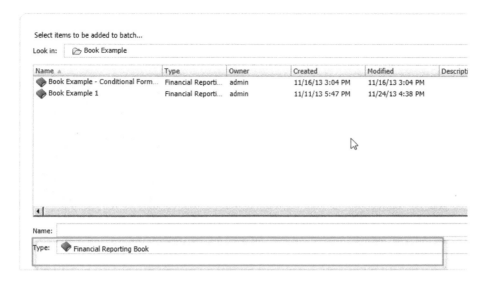

The batch object is the same whether it contains books or reports, and both books and reports can be included in the same batch. Once the batch object is saved, the batch containing the book is scheduled in the same order the batch of reports was scheduled.

In this example, the scheduled batch is called Conditional Book Batch. The book configuration impacts the Point of Views available in the batch. The following screenshot shows the details behind the book.

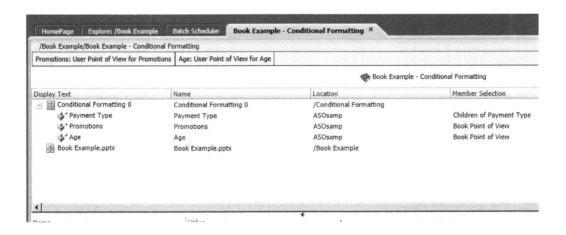

Notice the book has a Children function for Payment Type. When creating a scheduled batch, the Point of View configuration window does not show a POV option for Payment Type since it already contains a definition for the member. The following screenshot shows the first configuration window for the batch containing the book.

In this example, no changes are made to the Point of View. Continuing with the setup, the batch output is configured to run in the same folder with the batch file for simplicity.

Pressing Next on the output configuration screen and then Finish on the final screen sets the batch to execute. Upon completion of the example, navigating to the output's folder location shows the Financial Reporting Snapshot Book.

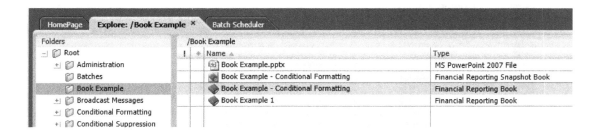

The **Financial Reporting Snapshot Book** is similar to the Financial Reporting Snapshot Report, where the entire output from the book is saved with the snapshot. The snapshot can be opened in HTML preview, PDF preview, or the complete book can be opened in PDF format. Opening the book in HTML preview displays as follows:

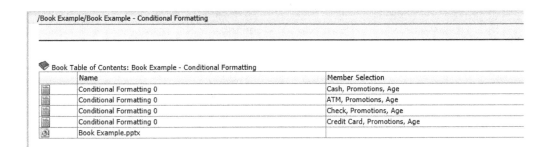

Notice the book executed a set of reports for the Children of the Payment Type node as configured in the book. Double-clicking an object in the book snapshot opens the completed report as shown here.

	Original Price	Price Paid	Variance
Digital Cameras	392.460	389.607	2,853
Camcorders	801,593	796,907	4,686
Photo Printers	403,432	400,169	3,263
Digital Cameras/Camcorders	1,597,485	1,586,683	10,802
Handhelds	#MISSING	#MISSING	#ERROR
Memory	748,086	742,454	5,633
Other Accessories	1,869,402	1,857,971	11,431
Handhelds/PDAs	2,617,488	2,600,425	17,063
Boomboxes	501,797	498,277	3,519
Radios	490,492	487,417	3,074
Portable Audio	992,288	985,695	6,594
Personal Electronics	5,207,261	5,172,803	34,458
Direct View	#MISSING	#MISSING	#ERROR
Projection TVs	566,620	563,567	3,053
Flat Panel	423,693	420,531	3,161
HDTV	1,525,650	1,516,513	9,137

Example: Advanced Batching Using a Burst File

Basic batch configuration provides limited features for controlling individual outputs. The use of a **Bursting File**, however, provides the means to store burst file parameters in a separate text file and designate a specific output configuration for each parameter.

The same report utilized throughout the chapter is utilized in a new batch saved with the name Advanced Exporting Batch. A new scheduled batch called Advanced Exporting Example was created to schedule the batch job. In the example, a Bursting List file is utilized to override the exporting features of the interface, and used to perform burst file-specific operations including email, security, and output locations.

After modifying the batch and authenticating, the first screen of the batch configuration interface displays the configured options.

Notice the batch is set to run immediately upon finalization and the two Point of View entries are set to the top level. Also note that the Bursting Options are selected for Payment Type with members selected. Instead of moving to the next screen, the Preview Bursting List button is selected opening the Preview Bursting List window shown in the following screenshots below.

Preview Bursting List

Payment Type	Subfolder Name	Financial Reporting Object Name
Cash	<<FinancialReportingObjectName()>>-<<MemberName()>>	<<FinancialReportingObjectName()
ATM	<<FinancialReportingObjectName()>>-<<MemberName()>>	<<FinancialReportingObjectName()
Check	<<FinancialReportingObjectName()>>-<<MemberName()>>	<<FinancialReportingObjectName()
Credit Card	<<FinancialReportingObjectName()>>-<<MemberName()>>	<<FinancialReportingObjectName()

Export

	Email Addresses	Group Names	Role Names	User Names	External Root Folder for PDF
>>					
>>					
>>					
>>					

Notice the first column of the file is the name of the dimension selected for bursting, and the members selected in the interface populates down the rows. This preview file is utilized to show the format of the exported file. The following information describes the burst file fields:

- Dimension Name – The first column is used to specify the values for bursting. These values must match dimension values in the application or the bursting file skips invalid members. Only member names can be used. Functions and lists are not allowed.

- Subfolder Name – This is the name of the subfolder that receives the file. The subfolder is created inside the folder location set in the snapshot export settings. The subfolder can be set to a custom folder name, providing the ability to group the report output into separate folders, as desired, with separate permissions.

- Financial Reporting Object Name – Names of each snapshot file.

- Email Address – The email address of the recipients receiving the bursting email if PDF email output is configured.

- Group Names, Role Names, and User Names – This feature provides the ability to apply permissions to each export file and subfolder.

- External Root Folder for PDF – The location of the external shared drive folder receiving the PDF export.

The template for the burst file can be exported to the local machine from the system. Selecting the Export button on the preview interface prompts for a location to save the template to the local machine. After saving the file to the local directory, the file can be opened in text format or MS Excel and populated with content. The specific configuration in the following screenshot is used in this example. When the batch runs, the job executes the batch for each value in rows 2 through the end of the file.

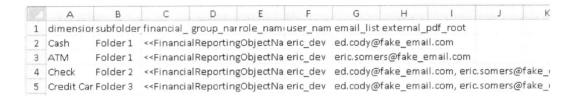

	A	B	C	D	E	F	G	H	I	J	K
1	dimensior	subfolder	financial_	group_nar	role_nam	user_nam	email_list	external_pdf_root			
2	Cash	Folder 1	<<FinancialReportingObjectNa			eric_dev	ed.cody@fake_email.com				
3	ATM	Folder 1	<<FinancialReportingObjectNa			eric_dev	eric.somers@fake_email.com				
4	Check	Folder 2	<<FinancialReportingObjectNa			eric_dev	ed.cody@fake_email.com, eric.somers@fake_				
5	Credit Car	Folder 3	<<FinancialReportingObjectNa			eric_dev	ed.cody@fake_email.com, eric.somers@fake_				

Note the subfolder, user_name, and email_list are configured with specific information. After the file configuration is complete, the file must be imported into Workspace before the file can be imported into the scheduled batch. It is recommended to keep the bursting file in the same location as the batch file for organizational purposes. Importing the file is achieved by selecting Import → File from the Workspace File menu as shown in the following screenshot.

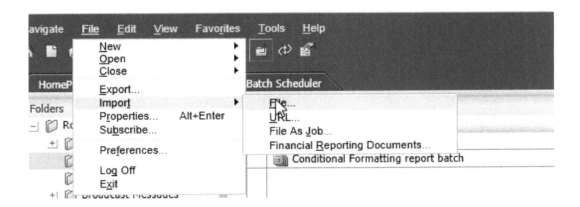

After locating and selecting the file on the local machine, selecting open brings up the import options for importing a file. After finalizing the import and verifying the file name, pressing Finish imports the file into the selected location. After the file upload is complete, the scheduled batch must be edited to take advantage of the burst file.

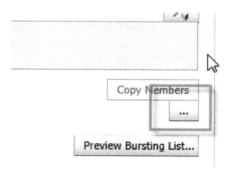

Schedule Batch ✕

Start Time

Frequency

Perform Now ▾

Start Date | End Date
Jan 18, 2014 ▾ | Jan 18, 2014 ▾

Start Time | Time Zone
⬍ | ▾

Scheduled Batch Point of View

| Payment Type: Payment Type | Promotions: Promotions | Age: Age | | ‹ | › |

Bursting Options

☑ Run batch for multiple members in the dimension:

Payment Type ▾

Select Members 🔍

Cash, ATM, Check, Credit Card

Bursting File | Copy Members
| ...
| Preview Bursting List...

Help | Back | Next | Cancel

The burst file is selected by pressing the ... button on the interface.

Upon pressing the ... button, a window appears asking the user to select the burst file. Navigating to the location of the burst file, selecting the file, and pressing OK loads the file into the scheduler window as shown in the following screenshot.

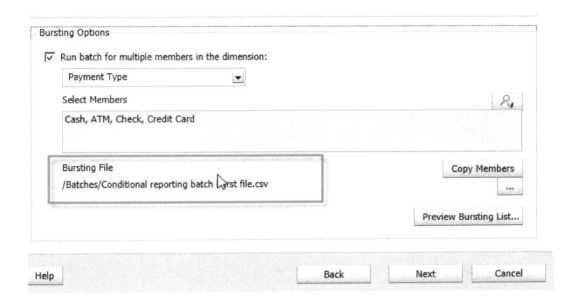

The Bursting File section of the window now shows the path and selected burst file. Selecting the Preview Bursting List button now shows the uploaded values. Click OK to close the preview window and then select Next to continue with scheduling the batch. Since this example includes emailing the report results to specific people, the Export as PDF option and the Email as PDF Attachments option must be selected.

Pressing Next opens the PDF Attachment Email window for selecting the list of email users. The appearance of the PDF Attachment Screen might seem counter-intuitive since an email burst file is being used, but a user *MUST* be added to the Batch Recipient List line for this to work as shown.

In the Message Subject line, an appropriate email subject can be typed in. In the message body section, an email message can be added.

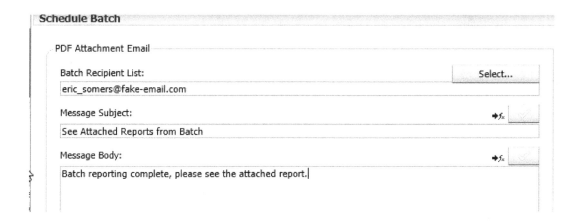

Click the Preview Bursting List button again:

	Email Addresses	G
>>	eric_somers@fake-email.com,eric.somers@fake_email.com	
>>	eric_somers@fake-email.com,ed.cody@fake_email.com	
>>	eric_somers@fake-email.com,eric.somers@fake_email.com	
>>	eric_somers@fake-email.com,ed.cody@fake_email.com	

Notice that the eric_somers recipient is now inserted into every single row of the burst file along with the other emails previously specified. As previously mentioned, in order to get email bursting to work, a recipient MUST be added in the PDF Attachment Email screen. A best practice recommendation is to set this email to the person that configures the batches so they receive all of the reports in the event of needing to troubleshoot an error.

After configuring the final interface for successful and failed messages, selecting Finish executes the batch with the bursting list. When the batch completes, the batches are exported, folders created, and emails sent based on the file definitions. The following screenshot displays the folder structure and folder permissions after the burst execution.

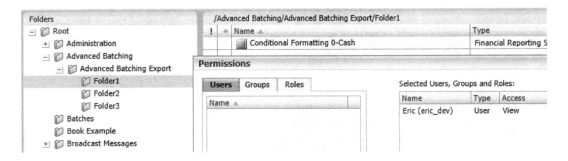

Each report is put into defined folders and defined users are provided with View access on both the folders and reports.

Summary

Financial Reporting Batches provide automated functionality for running reports across input parameters. The feature takes advantage of the automated scheduling utility that is built into the Oracle EPM system, providing a web user interface for scheduling and managing content.

The chapter started with an overview of creating a batch file in Workspace. With a batch file created, an overview of the configuration options for configuring the batch was demonstrated. These options include the configuration of schedule, frequency, member selection, and bursting. Reporting output features were discussed at length with a preview of the reporting snapshot HTML and PDF outputs. The chapter transitioned into the methods used to monitor job status with an overview of reviewing the job log files and viewing the output saved with the finished job. The chapter provided examples of using both a financial report and a book in batch files, with the configuration of Point of View selections. The chapter concluded with the advanced batching concept using a bursting file for customizing the output location, features, and permissions for each individual output file.

12

Oracle Smart View Integration with Financial Reporting

One of the most unique functions of the Oracle EPM product suite is the integration of the **Smart View** add-in for MS Office across all Hyperion applications and, now, Oracle Business Intelligence. Smart View provides the ability to pull Hyperion Financial reports into MS Office applications and easily refresh content. Specific functions for Excel, PowerPoint, and Word exist, with Excel integration providing both fully-formatted content importing, and the ability to drill into the content shown in each grid through the query-ready feature. Excel's features provide a way to directly interface with the application for the purpose of building and enriching deliverables as well as performing analysis.

The following topics are introduced in this chapter:

- The Smart View Ribbon
- Reporting & Analysis in Excel
- Microsoft Excel & Query-Ready Mode
- Microsoft Word & PowerPoint Integration
- Copy & Paste Smart View Feature

The Smart View Ribbon

Since Oracle Smart View is an add-in to Microsoft Office, the application functions directly inside MS Office applications and adds a new ribbon to the application. The application is downloadable from Workspace and is commonly distributed or pushed out to all Hyperion application users. In Word, PowerPoint, and Excel, the new Smart View ribbon is added to the list of menus as shown in the following screenshot.

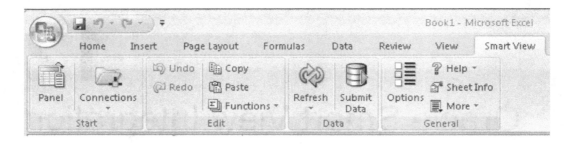

The Smart View ribbon displayed above is the ribbon for Excel. The Excel ribbon is slightly different from the Word and PowerPoint ribbons due to the additional functionality provided for ad-hoc querying, analysis, and other specific application features. Word and PowerPoint versions have a similar ribbon with functionality which is specific to refreshing application content into a document or presentation.

The first button on the ribbon is the Panel, which brings up a menu on the right-hand side of the page. The panel provides navigation to application content and features. Two types of connections exist: shared and private. In this example, the shared method is used, as it is typically the primary method for most environments. The connection string for shared connections is stored in the general options of Smart View. Smart View options are located by pressing the Options button on the ribbon. The following screenshot displays the location of the URL for shared connections.

General		(i)
Shared Connections URL:	http://hyperionpc:9000/workspace/SmartViewPr	▼
Number of Undo Actions	9	
Number of Most Recently Used items	9	
Delete All MRU Items		

Once the URL is entered, pressing the Panel button opens the Smart View Connection Window. The first screen of the panel is shown in the screenshot below.

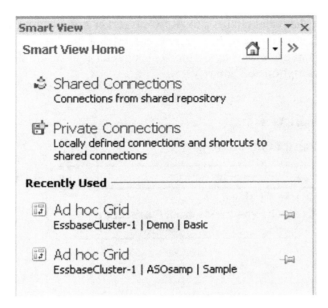

Clicking the Shared Connections button opens the authentication menu for logging into the system. Authorization for the application is completed using the same username and password that is used to login to the web interface. The screenshot below displays the login interface. For reference, notice that the shared connections URL is displayed below the connection buttons.

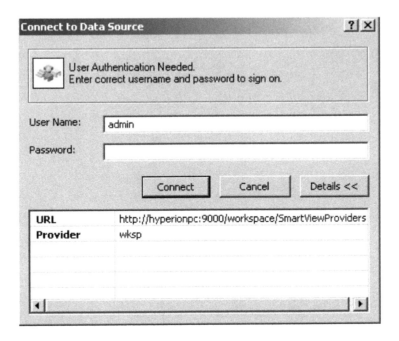

Once authenticated, the panel changes to show the server options available for the environment. In this environment, Essbase, Planning, and the Reporting and Analysis Framework are the server options available. This chapter focuses on the Reporting and Analysis Framework options of Smart View.

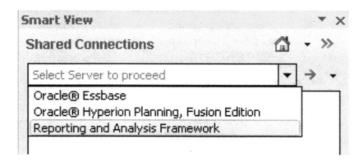

Reporting & Analysis in Microsoft Excel

One of the most unique features of Smart View is the ability to browse Workspace from the Smart View interface. Selecting the Reporting and Analysis Framework from the list of available options opens a connection to the configured servers. Expanding the server node displays the folder structure of Workspace. Since the same security is applied in Smart View as logging into the application from the web, users are only presented with folders and objects available to the specific user.

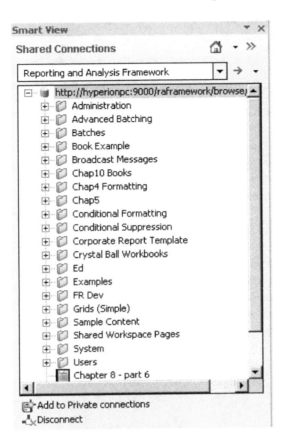

The following screenshot shows the Explore window of the Workspace drilled into a folder of reports.

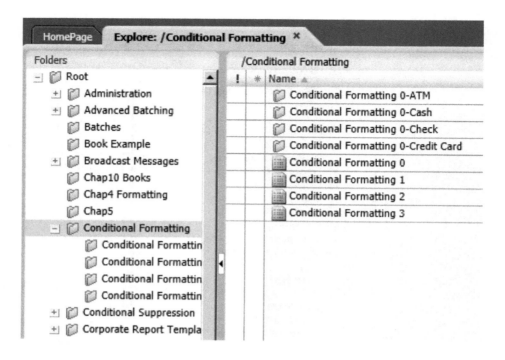

Expanding the Smart View panel, similarly, displays the same list of reports:

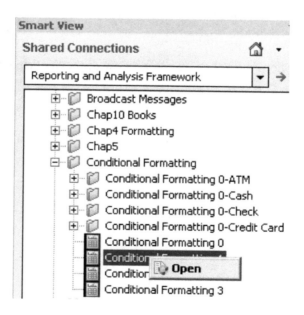

Right-clicking on a report brings up a menu with the option to open the report. Opening the report displays a preview window that contains options for importing the object into the interface. The preview window starts with the user Point of View (if one exists) as shown in the following screenshot.

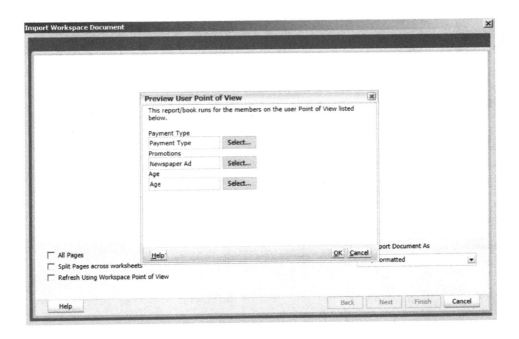

Excel in Fully-Formatted Mode

When a report is open in Microsoft Excel, there are a few additional import options which are not available when working with Word and PowerPoint. In Excel, a report's contents can be imported into the spreadsheet in a Fully Formatted or Query Ready format. The Word and PowerPoint import features only provide an image import option. The following screenshot displays the preview window for a report open in Excel.

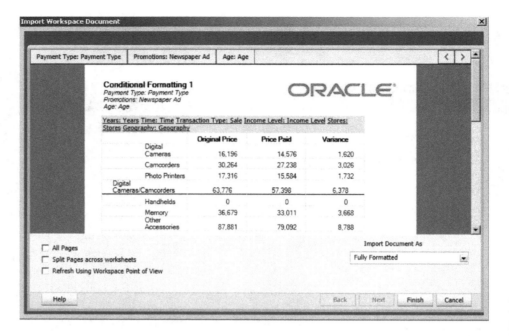

The following options are displayed at the bottom of the screen which controls the import options:

- **All Pages** – This selection is used when a page prompt is included in the report. If there is no page prompt, the option does not apply. If there is a page prompt and the user does not check All Pages, the import only displays the current page selection.

- **Split Pages across worksheets** – splits each page of the report into a separate Excel tab. If a page prompt applies, each page prompt value is exported as a separate tab.

- **Refresh Using Workspace Point of View** – This option refreshes the report using the Point of View definitions setup by the user in Workspace.

On the bottom right side of the interface, a drop-down appears with document import formatting options. The first option, **Fully Formatted**, opens the report in Excel with all of the formatting retained. The text and numeric values of the report are imported into Excel as text and numeric values in the cells, and Excel formatting is applied to each cell to mimic the formatting displayed on the web. The following screenshot demonstrates a fully-formatted report imported into Excel.

		Original Price	Price Paid	Variance
	Conditional Formatting 1			
	Payment Type: Payment Type			
	Promotions: Newspaper Ad			
	Age: Age			
	Digital Cameras	16,196	14,576	1,620
	Camcorders	30,264	27,238	3,026
	Photo Printers	17,316	15,584	1,732
	Digital Cameras/Camcorders	63,776	57,398	6,378
	Handhelds	0	0	0
	Memory	36,679	33,011	3,668
	Other Accessories	87,881	79,092	8,788
	Handhelds/PDAs	124,560	112,104	12,456
	Boomboxes	20,330	18,297	2,033
	Radios	23,147	20,833	2,314
	Portable Audio	43,477	39,130	4,347
	Personal Electronics	**231,812**	**208,632**	**23,181**
	Direct View	0	0	0
	Projection TVs	48,960	44,064	4,896
	Flat Panel	18,508	16,657	1,851

Note: When a report is opened in Smart View in fully formatted mode, a logo placed in the right-hand corner of the screen may move from its originally intended location. Placing a logo on the left-hand side of the page aligns better when refreshing reports in Excel.

Once the report is imported into the Excel file, it is easily refreshed by pressing the refresh button on the Smart View ribbon. The following screenshot displays the refresh button with the available options.

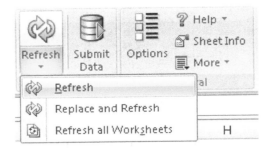

Once the refresh is complete, the application displays the number of pages refreshed in the workbook.

Editing the Point of View

After an object is imported into Excel, the object may be edited without completely reimporting the object. The Connections button on the Smart View toolbar contains the settings for modifying both the data displayed as well as the connection to the application. The following screenshot shows the Smart View ribbon open to the connection options.

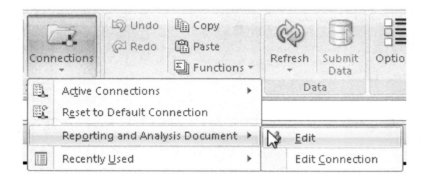

Selecting the object and then selecting the Connections → Report and Analysis Document → Edit button opens the Financial Reporting preview window for setting the Point of View for the reporting object – similar to importing a new reporting object.

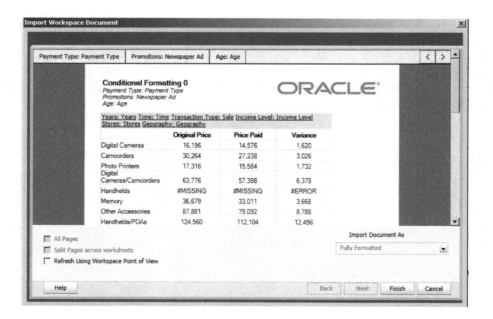

After making the desired selections and clicking Finish, the updated report is imported into the Excel document with the updated content.

Excel Query-Ready Mode

A unique feature of Financial Reporting is the instant conversion of a report grid into an active query-ready sheet. **Query-Ready Mode** refers to the capability of converting a standard reporting grid into an Excel template with the ability to connect to the Hyperion application and instantly drill into data. This conversion preps the Excel file with the correct dimensional layout for the rows, columns, and Point of View. In reports with multiple grids, each visible grid used in the report is drillable. Rows and columns of formulas are excluded. Query-Ready Mode can be accessed both through the HTML view of a Financial Report on the web as well as by importing a Financial Report into Excel through Smart View. The query-ready feature facilitates the ability to drill-down into the data view in the report, adding the means to perform detailed analysis on the data returned in the grid.

Query-Ready Mode in HTML

The HTML report viewing option is a way to invoke the query-ready mode directly from the report display. Unlike the PDF view, the HTML view contains an additional set of text at the bottom right-hand side of each grid called **Export In Query-Ready Mode** as shown in the following screenshot.

CD/DVD drives	0	0	0
Computers and Peripherals	63,190	56,871	6,319
Other	**63,190**	**56,871**	**6,319**

Export In Query-Ready Mode

Conditional Formatting 1   Company Confidential   Page: 1 of 1
Run by: admin

When selected, Microsoft Excel is launched and the rows, columns, pages and Point of View are converted into the ad-hoc analysis format for Essbase. An active connection to the Essbase application is also established providing a means to work directly with the data in the application. An example of the conversion is shown in the following screenshot.

	A	B	C	D	E
2		Original Price	Price Paid	POV [Book2] ▼ ✕	
3	Digital Cameras	16196	14576.4	Years	▼
4	Camcorders	30264	27237.6	Time	▼
5	Photo Printers	17316	15584.4	Sale	▼
6	Digital Cameras/Camcorders	63776	57398.4	Payment Type	▼
7	Handhelds	0	0	Newspaper Ad	▼
8	Memory	36679	33011.1	Age	▼
9	Other Accessories	87880.5	79092.45	Income Level	▼
10	Handhelds/PDAs	124559.5	112103.55	Stores	▼
11	Boomboxes	20329.5	18296.55	Geography	▼
12	Radios	23147.25	20833.23		
13	Portable Audio	43476.75	39129.78	Refresh ⓘ	
14	Personal Electronics	231812.25	208631.73		
15	Direct View	0	0		
16	Projection TVs	48960	44064		

Smart View Query-Ready Importing

The second method of executing a query-ready sheet is by importing the report using the Smart View **Query-Ready** function. When opening a report using Smart View, switching the import settings to Query-Ready sets the grid to import into an ad-hoc query-ready sheet. The following screenshot shows the import drop-down set to Query-Ready.

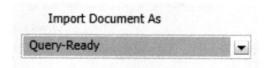

Upon finishing the import, each grid is imported into a separate Excel worksheet in the following format.

	A	B	C	D	E	F	G	H	I
1	Years	Time	Sale	Payment Type	Newspaper Ad	Age	Income Level	Stores	Geograp
2		Original Price	Price Paid						
3	Digital Cameras	16196	14576						
4	Camcorders	30264	27238						
5	Photo Printers	17316	15584						
6	Digital Cameras/Camcorders	63776	57398						
7	Handhelds	0	0						
8	Memory	36679	33011						
9	Other Accessories	87881	79092						
10	Handhelds/PDAs	124560	112104						
11	Boomboxes	20330	18297						
12	Radios	23147	20833						
13	Portable Audio	43477	39130						
14	Personal Electronics	231812	208632						
15	Direct View	0	0						
16	Projection TVs	48960	44064						
17	Flat Panel	18508	16657						
18	HDTV	87225	78503						
19	Stands	23793	21413						
20	Televisions	178485	160637						
21	Home Theater	19730	17757						

The direct import method through Smart View is slightly different from the HTML query-ready method, where the connection back to the application is neither established nor active upon import. In this case, the user must browse the Smart View panel to the application and then select Ad-hoc Analysis. When selected, the sheet activates for querying and converts the blue highlighted cells back to white. The Point of View is configured and the sheet is ready for ad-hoc analysis as shown in the following screenshot.

	A	B	C	D
2		Original Price	Price Paid	POV Conditio ▼ ✕
3	Digital Cameras	16196	14576.4	Years ▼
4	Camcorders	30264	27237.6	Time ▼
5	Photo Printers	17316	15584.4	Sale ▼
6	Digital Cameras/Camcorders	63776	57398.4	
7	Handhelds	#Missing	#Missing	Payment Type ▼
8	Memory	36679	33011.1	Newspaper Ad ▼
9	Other Accessories	87880.5	79092.45	Age ▼
10	Handhelds/PDAs	124559.5	112103.55	Income Level ▼
11	Boomboxes	20329.5	18296.55	Stores ▼
12	Radios	23147.25	20833.23	Geography ▼
13	Portable Audio	43476.75	39129.78	Refresh ⓘ
14	Personal Electronics	231812.25	208631.73	
15	Direct View	#Missing	#Missing	
16	Projection TVs	48960	44064	
17	Flat Panel	18507.5	16656.75	
18	HDTV	87225	78502.5	
19	Stands	23792.5	21413.25	
20	Televisions	178485	160636.5	

Microsoft Word & PowerPoint Integration

Refreshing application content directly into a Word document or PowerPoint presentation is a desirable and useful feature provided by Smart View and its integration with Financial Reporting. While Excel provides a set of import format capabilities for importing and querying Financial Reporting documents, Word and PowerPoint provide the ability to import report images into documents and presentations. The images may be resized or moved, and text can be placed around the image as desired. The images may even be cropped, allowing for sections of a full report to display in the output. The images imported from Financial Reporting maintain a link back to the system, providing the ability to refresh a single image or all of the images from the Smart View toolbar. The feature provides a means to create reporting images specifically for use in deliverables with the aim of embedding active content directly into the finalized product.

Word & PowerPoint Smart View Ribbon

The Smart View ribbon for Word and PowerPoint is similar to the Excel ribbon and contains a set of options for working with Financial Reports and application content. The following screenshot displays the Smart View ribbon for Word and PowerPoint.

When creating an import, the first step is to navigate and select the object for import. Selecting the panel button opens a similar panel to the one seen when working with Excel. In this example, a report displaying a chart object is imported into PowerPoint. The following screenshot shows the Smart View Panel opened to the report location.

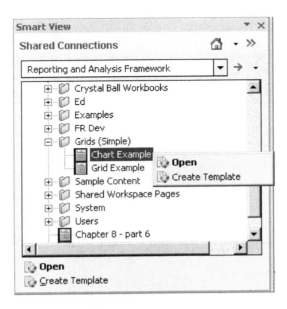

The Financial Reporting preview window appears for selecting the Point of View and settings as shown next.

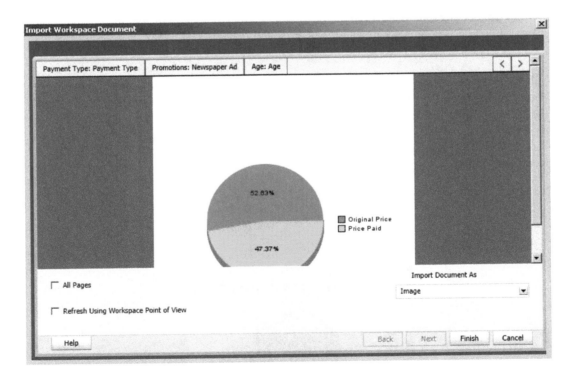

If page prompts are used, the imported file points to the selected page. Selecting the All Pages checkbox on the import page imports each page into a separate slide in PowerPoint or separate page in Word. Notice, at the top of the preview page, that there is a way to set the Point of View for the report. Once set and finished, the report imports into the application. The following screenshot displays the chart imported into PowerPoint.

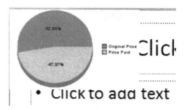

One nice feature of Smart View and Financial Reporting integration is the automatic removal of unnecessary whitespace from an image. Notice the preview window contained a large amount of whitespace at the top of the report image. When imported into PowerPoint, the image is cropped to remove all of the unnecessary whitespace.

When imported, the image is moved to a new slide and placed in the upper left-hand corner of the page. Each imported image may be cut and pasted into desired application locations without losing server connection information. Text and other application sections may be placed around the application image. The following screenshot shows a PowerPoint slide configured with a title and bullets in a text body with the Financial Reporting image.

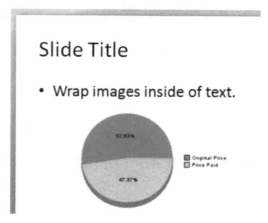

Refreshing Application Content

At any time, a single slide or all slides in a document can be refreshed with new application content through the use of the Refresh button on the Smart View toolbar. The following image shows the refresh button along with the options for refreshing.

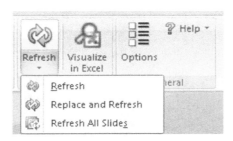

Each time a refresh is executed or an application object changed, the application prompts with the number of pages updated as shown in the following screenshot.

Editing the Point of View

After an object is imported into a Word or PowerPoint file, the object may be edited in a similar fashion to editing an imported report in Excel. The Connections button on the Smart View toolbar contains the settings for modifying both the data displayed and the connection to the application. The following screenshot shows the Smart View ribbon open to the connection options.

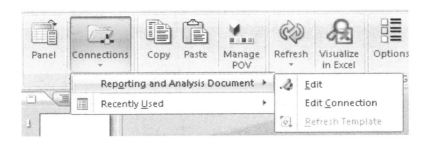

Selecting the object and then selecting Connections → Report and Analysis Document → Edit opens the Financial Reporting preview window for setting the Point of View for the reporting object – similar to importing a new reporting object.

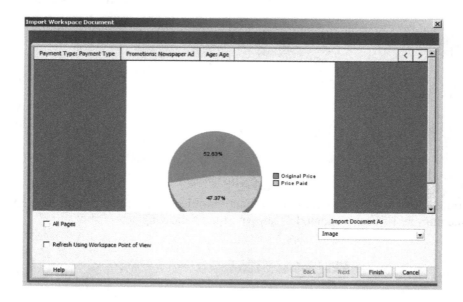

After making changes to the object, clicking Finish imports the new definitions into the image and the image updates accordingly. The image does not change in size, shape, or location so the presentation layout remains unaltered.

Smart View Copy and Paste Functionality

One other feature worth nothing in this section is the additional **Copy** and **Paste** buttons that are contained on the Smart View toolbar. These buttons are separate from the copy and paste buttons contained in the standard Office applications and apply to copying and pasting application definitions across applications. The following screenshot shows the copy and paste buttons from the Excel Smart View ribbon.

Note the ability to browse more than just reporting and analysis objects from the Word and PowerPoint panel. In this case, an ad-hoc analysis can be opened from PowerPoint.

When opening an ad-hoc from PowerPoint, the Excel application is launched with an active connection to the selected application. Once the data cells of interest are selected, they can be copied and pasted from the Excel application into Word or PowerPoint. The following screenshot shows two values from the sample application copied using the Excel Smart View Copy button.

B3		▼	f_x	38020539.25	
	A	B	C	D	E
1		Payment Type	Promotions	Age	Income Level
2		Current Year	Previous Year		
3	Measures	38020539.25	73416391.5		

When the data cells are brought over to Word or PowerPoint by utilizing the Paste button on the Smart View ribbon in the respective applications, each pasted numeric cell is created as a separate object with the text #NEED_REFRESH. This configuration is similar to an HSGetCell Excel formula query and requires a refresh from the Smart View toolbar. The cells contain the intersection of all of the dimensions as well as connection information. Once the refresh button is pressed or a refresh takes place, the data from the live application is queried and displayed; dynamic text labels update directly from the application.

PowerPoint *before* refresh:

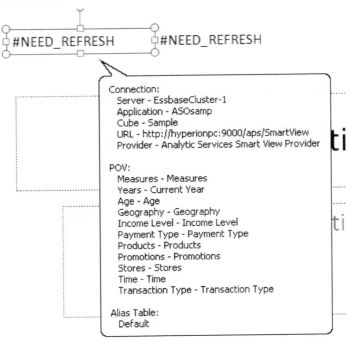

Notice how highlighting a field displays information and the intersection of the value.

Power Point *after* refresh:

38020539.25   73416391.5

Word *before* refresh:

Sample Numbers: #NEED_REFRESH #NEED_REFRESH

Word *after* refresh:

Sample Numbers: 38020539.25   73416391.5

Summary

Smart View furthers the efficacy of Financial Reporting, providing the capability to import dynamic application content into final deliverables and drill into reporting content to view data variances.

The chapter started with an introduction to the Smart View ribbon for Excel and the features used for importing reporting content. The fully formatted import method was demonstrated as was the method to refresh the report once it was imported into the Excel application.

The next capability demonstrated was query-ready accessibility. Query-ready mode provides a way to drill into displayed content in each report grid, providing an additional level of analysis. Methods for accessing the query-ready mode through HTML and Smart View were demonstrated along with differences to each approach. The chapter then transitioned to working with Smart View in PowerPoint and Word. Importing reports into final deliverables was discussed along with the features for refreshing image content and editing an image post-import. Finally, the chapter touched on the ability to copy and paste numbers from an active Excel connection into Word and PowerPoint, supplying the means to refresh numbers from the application into fully-formatted text to further add dynamic content into each document.

Index

Index

Index

The Oracle Data Relationship Management 11 Guide is aimed at DRM developers and business users, and focuses on providing an understanding of the product whilst acclimating users to the software. It provides an in-depth understanding on how to integrate DRM's powerful functionality into an operational business environment.

> Learn the Steps Needed to Accomplish Master Data Management Project Success
> Build a DRM Data Model with Hierarchies, Properties, and Validations
> Integrate DRM with Upstream and Downstream Systems
> Explore the Data Relationship Governance Workflow Module
> Learn the Methods behind Application Maintenance and Migrations

The latest version of Java offers numerous improvements and new features to better utilize Java. Streams, for example, supports a fluent approach to problem solving and lets the developer take advantage of concurrency with minimal effort, whilst Lambda Expressions offer new ways of expressing a solution that brings efficiency and succinct programming.

> Learn how interface enhancements - such as default methods - affect new additions to Java 8 and their impact on multiple inheritance between interfaces
> Use lambda expressions to simplify solutions to development problems
> Discover how the new Stream interface supports query type problems
> Explore the new support for concurrent processing including that supported by Streams
> Find out why the new date and time enhancements make working with time so much easier than it used to be
> Includes information on the Nashorn JavaScript Engine, File IO Enhancements, and Project Jigsaw

The Oracle Siebel Open UI Developer's Handbook shows experienced Siebel developers how to get the very most out of the new Open UI framework, quickly and effectively!

In the book, covering Innovation Packs 2013 and 2014, you will:

> Learn all about Siebel's Open UI Architecture
> Create Custom Presentation Models and Physical Renderers
> Understand how to apply Custom Styles and Themes
> Customize and Deploy Siebel Mobile Applications

> Integrate Siebel Open UI with external Applications

Written by distinguished Siebel CRM experts from Oracle, the book is filled with practical information and exclusive insights.

Aimed at newcomers to the world of exceptions, assertions and logging, this book cuts-to-the-chase in a logical and easy-to-understand manner. Get under the hood and find out about declaring, throwing and catching exceptions; what checked and unchecked exceptions mean; how to define custom exception classes; why (and how) you should use assertions; the value and power of logging; and much more!

> Learn about the different Types of Exception, and how to deal with them elegantly
> Dig deep into Exception Objects and learn how to Define Custom Exceptions

> Discover practical guidelines on the effective use of Exceptions, including when to chain Exceptions
> Sanity check your application code, using simple pass/fail Assertion tests
> Get to grips with java.util.logging, Log4J, and other logging frameworks
> Filled with lots of sample code, hints, tips and notes. Download the code from this website for free.

CPSIA information can be obtained
at www.ICGtesting.com
Printed in the USA
LVHW061348180320
650444LV00004B/50

9 780957 410534